THE WEAVER'S WAY

WHAT AN ANCIENT ART CAN TEACH YOU ABOUT YOUR APPROACH TO SHAPING CHANGE

CORRINA GRACE

INGENIUM BOOKS

PRAISE FOR THE WEAVER'S WAY

"Masterful, powerful, transformative. *The Weaver's Way* is a must read, I should say a must-travel! It transports you to an inner and outward journey of this complex world we live in, it empowers you through the privilege of meeting, and learning from, wonderful characters, who are in fact true leaders with powerful leadership, humility, and vulnerability lessons to share. It exposes you to enlightening practical exercises that will deepen your knowledge of your own soul and will help you re-shape your destiny and impact. Most importantly, it reminds you in a poignant way of how our art is our salvation, how humanity is interconnected, and how we can only survive crisis and challenges and make sustainable change as a collective."

— CHADIA EL MEOUCHI NAOUM, ASPEN GLOBAL
LEADERSHIP NETWORK

"Strategies for the healing our world needs today. If you are searching for a book that guides you towards collective leadership, you will find it in the stories in *The Weaver's Way*."

— LOUISE TARRIER, CARBON POSITIVE AUSTRALIA

"...one of the most remarkable, beautiful , practical, and inspiring books on community-based change I've yet to encounter."

— MARGARET WHEATLEY, *LEADERSHIP AND THE NEW SCIENCE* AND *WHO DO WE CHOOSE TO BE?*

"Through storytelling and reflection, The Weaver's Way offers us a path of liberation – leading us toward connectedness and collective well-being. It is much-needed medicine for our challenging times."

"Brilliant, moving, and inspiring."

"...a map, field guide, and practical how-to to create the future we are all craving for. A practical primer for those stepping into their everyday leadership and those who with the prompt of a great question will step over the threshold and find themselves leading. For those more comfortable in their leadership skins, you will find stories to encourage you and remind you that you too are part of a tidal wave of leaders transforming the world."

Published by Ingenium Books Publishing Inc.
Toronto, Ontario, Canada M6P 1Z2
www.ingeniumbooks.com

International Standard Book Numbers (ISBNs)
eBook: 978-1-990688-08-9
Paperback: 978-1-990688-07-2

Editing by Jennifer Crosswhite.
Cover design by Jessica Bell Designs.

The author and publisher acknowledge with gratitude the permissions granted to reproduce the copyrighted material in this book.

CONTENTS

To Abigail, Loida, and all the other weavers near and far.

Thank you.

INTRODUCTION

A FLOOD, A VOLCANO, AND A WHOLE NEW FUTURE

The rain was relentless—the kind of steady downpour that makes you wonder how the sky can possibly hold that much water. It had been coming down hard and fast all weekend, topping off what had been a wet and soggy February. The tin roof hummed from the barrage of heavy droplets—a low-throated sound that normally evoked a comforting feeling of being home. Today, however, the non-stop battery was exhausting—an audible assault that strained the nerves and left me feeling weary without having done much at all since it was too wet—the ground boggy and the roads too slick to do much more than hunker down inside.

I was staying at my mum's house in the Northern Rivers of New South Wales (NSW)—an area that is no stranger to floods. But this. This was different. Certainly nothing that I'd experienced in my lifetime. For a number of days, rain gauges across the region had read daily rainfalls in excess of 200 mm (over seven inches). And it wasn't stopping.

As I headed to bed that Sunday evening I paused in the doorway to my mum's bedroom where she lay on the bed, anxiously scrolling through weather alerts and news updates. "Here we go again," she said, as she looked up at me. "Lismore's going to cop it."

"Yeah…I don't know, Mum," I replied, mirroring the worry written across her face. "I think this is going to be a big one."

And it was. In the twenty-four hours to 9 a.m. on Monday, February 28, a rain gauge at Dunoon—one of the small communities in the Lismore catchment area—recorded 775 mm (over thirty inches) of rain. The second highest rainfall ever recorded in NSW. Waking up at just over 5 a.m. that Monday, the ever-present sound of rain quickly reminded me of the sense of unease with which I'd gone to sleep the night before. I quickly switched on the local news radio, searching for updates. I showered, made a cup of tea, and had just sat down at my computer when the radio presenter introduced someone from the local emergency services.

"The river's flowing hard and rising fast," he told the presenter, "and we need to evacuate people quickly. The SES doesn't have enough resources to do it, so if you've got a boat, we need you out there."

I got up from my desk and walked out into the hallway. The light in my mum's room was on. Unusual for this hour, she was already awake and listening to the same news broadcast. "How many people on your street have boats?" I asked her.

"Two," she replied. "One across the road, and one up and around the corner."

"Okay," I said, "I'm going to grab some things and go knock on their doors. We need to get out there."

I struggle for the words to describe that day. I want to say that it was a blur, but that feels contradictory to the jarring scenes that replayed in my mind for weeks afterward whenever I tried to sleep. Maybe the *blur* I'm looking for is more about speed. Nonstop movement. No time for thought between action and reaction, everything going so quickly: the water, the boats, the people, the debris. A town being swept away.

Our first rescue that morning was on the south side of town, which is always the first to go under. To get there we had to first cross the central business district, navigating around overhead power lines (now underwater) that threatened to tangle the boat's propeller, and then cross the point where two angry, swollen rivers converged. Just before crossing over we stopped, pulling the boat up onto the top of the bridge, just visible above the water, so we could untangle a mess of plastic and rope that had wrapped around the propeller.

Getting across the river, the scale of what was happening finally hit me. Every landmark I knew was gone, replaced by a roiling brown expanse dotted with an archipelago of treetops, power poles, and tin roofs. All around us, people were screaming from their rooftops or calling out from top story windows about who should be rescued as a priority—the elderly, people with mobility issues, families with small children. We had an address for a house where we'd been told there was a family with two young girls. With nothing other than the GPS on my phone to tell us where we were—the street signs and numbers having long ago lost themselves to the murky brown depths—we pulled up to the house, the water already halfway up the windows on the second floor.

As we pulled up, we began calling out. A neighbor standing on his verandah shouted out to us, saying that they'd climbed up into the roof space inside the house—a potentially deadly decision as the waters were still rising fast. Hanging on to the porch railing, I climbed out of the boat onto what I assumed was the second story verandah. The water was well above my waist. I waded inside the house, pushing aside toys, clothing, chairs, a kitchen table—a family's entire life floating around me. Just inside the hallway I met a man coming out carrying a young girl—perhaps seven or eight years old—her arms wrapped in a vicelike grip around his neck, screaming in terror. "Where are the others?" I asked, half shouting to be heard.

"Up in the roof space," he responded.

"Okay, pass her to me and go get them," I yelled. The little girl refused to let go. "It's okay, it's okay. I've got you," I told her, transferring the vise to my own neck. Her shaking was strong enough to make my own body begin to shiver in response. I waded back outside to the boat. "I'm going to keep you safe," I told her, hugging her tight. "We're all going to hop into this boat and go somewhere dry." As I passed her up to the driver, something behind the boat caught my eye: a cow, eyes rolling wildly, being dragged along by the flood water. I made a silent prayer that these wild waters wouldn't make a liar out of me and waded back into the house.

With everyone out of the house, I climbed back into the boat. As I did so, the driver grabbed my arm. "We're taking on water," he said, "we can't take anyone else or we may not make it back across the rivers." I gave a short, sharp nod of understanding. We pulled back out into the street, liquified as though by alchemy into a fast-flowing torrent, purging the town of all its possessions. All around us, people screamed out for help.

"We can't take any more," I yelled. "We'll come back for you."

By the time we made it back to where we had launched, our boat was done for, and so was the driver. "I'm out," he said. "Are you coming?" Quiet when we had left, the street had become as busy as a boat ramp on Saturday morning. Countless small aluminum fishing boats—which would later be dubbed "the tinny army"—coming and going as they discharged their cargo of wet and terrified people before heading back out. I shook my head. I wasn't going anywhere until it was over.

"Thanks for the boat," I told him. "You did a great job."

There is a concept in Buddhism, "warm hand to warm hand." It is a message about relationships: how wisdom, compassion, care are passed on, person to person. That day, even amidst the chaos and devastation, I was acutely aware of this concept at work as people were —quite literally—passed from hand-to-hand, lives enveloped into this web of generosity and love that had burst forth, spontaneous and unfettered. The human spirit in its purest form.

More than any other government agency or institution it was this web, in all its manifestations, that saved lives and soothed souls that day. There were rescues—hundreds of them. But there was also a hot coffee pressed into shaking hands, a jerry can of fuel handed off quickly between two passing boats, a dry shirt and rain jacket appearing out of nowhere and countless other kindnesses and acts of bravery that pulled the community through. Surrounded by strangers, I hadn't felt this connected for years. Perhaps not since the deadly eruption of Guatemala's Volcán de Fuego back in June 2018. But disturbingly, solidarity and human connection weren't the only things that those two disastrous events had in common. In the days and weeks that followed the flood I was haunted by other, less uplifting similarities.

The business-as-usual government and institutional responses—dominated by personal agendas and political positioning—were not only painfully inadequate and slow to respond, but at times were so blinded by their own bureaucracy and processes as to be laughable...if it wasn't so tragically painful for those on the receiving end. Battered and weary, with little left but their dignity, forced to face up to a system that says "yes, we'll take that too."

For those outside looking in, it is often a case of "me" at the expense of "we," our own need and desire to help overpowering our ability or willingness to listen. While undoubtedly well-intentioned, the outpouring of charity that comes after these types of events can be overwhelming. Community leaders turn to social media platforms to perform a delicate dance. Desperate not to offend, they thank people for their generosity while practically begging them to hold back and wait, as local volunteers struggle to deal with the huge influx of donated clothing and goods that the community is just not ready to receive.

And then, of course, there are those on the frontlines. Not leaders, but ordinary people doing extraordinary things. Stepping up tirelessly with grit and determination to gather the fraying threads of their community and weave them back together. I have built a career on supporting these kinds of local leaders who all-too-often are overlooked or undermined by traditional systems and the powers-that-be that question their authority and legitimacy, more focused on eroding trust and undermining these locally led efforts than actually creating real change.

But what is perhaps most unnerving about these two scenarios are not the similarities themselves, but the fact that Australia and Guatemala lie at opposite ends of the scale when it comes to indicators such as wealth, prosperity, and development. Yet in the chaotic aftermath, as the deep injustices of marginalization and poverty become only too apparent, none of that seems to make a difference.

The flooding on the east coast of Australia in early 2022 is a reminder that so-called "natural" disasters are just as much socio-political disasters: the interface between an extreme physical phenomenon and a human population, magnified by the vulnerability of that population. It is this reality that concerns me most about the impending climate crisis. Because if residents of a country that ranks number eight on the human development index, boasting the thirteenth largest economy in the world, are not immune...who amongst us really is?

As the cofounder of a UNESCO award-winning organization called SERES, where I now serve as a board member and senior advisor, I spent over a decade working in close proximity with impoverished and marginalized communities in Guatemala and El Salvador. I've lived in places where there is no justice. Where impunity reigns supreme and crimes of rape and murder go unpunished. Where a life is worth no more than a cell phone. Where a forest is destroyed or a river contaminated without a second thought, all in the name of profit. I've sat amongst the refuse of a society that sees people and the planet as disposable. The margins, they are called. And I used to believe that those margins were a long way from the hometown where I grew up. Now, I'm not so sure.

It's difficult not to feel alarmed. How is it that despite our best efforts, those margins continue to become wider and more crowded? Because the systems we have for solving these problems are woefully inadequate. Whether working on large systemic issues, tackling local challenges, or helping communities recover after a disaster—a new approach is needed. If the ten years that I spent living in Guatemala hadn't convinced me, then the ten days I spent back in northern NSW after the 2022 floods certainly have. None of us can afford to continue with business as usual.

THE "WE" IN *THE WEAVER'S WAY*

The framework I'm going to present to you in this book offers a different approach to problem solving and shaping change, drawn from my experiences working in those margins. I often refer to those margins as the frontlines, because that's what they feel like. A non-stop battle against poverty, pollution, violence, disease, discrimination, and insecurity. But those experiences are not what you might think. Because this isn't a story about hopelessness and helplessness but rather just the opposite. It's a story about agency and human dignity, and the incredible power of ordinary people ready and willing to do extraordinary things.

The Weaver's Way may challenge some of your fundamental views about how change happens. But it may also speak to an inner truth, nestled deep within the core of your being. An instinctive *knowing*, from whence comes the generosity, bravery, and goodness of the human spirit that is released, unhindered, during times of crisis.

My goal in *The Weaver's Way* is to make it easier for you to tap into this deeper, instinctive knowing so that it is accessible not just in times of crisis, but in your day-to-day actions and interactions. I knew that there were common threads that connected all the truly transformative, meaningful, and impactful change that I had seen over the years. But could I find the patterns?

It was a time for stillness. In the enforced isolation and stasis of COVID lockdowns, I took myself back to those frontlines. I explored the edges of memories – many of them painful. I remembered things I never knew I'd forgotten and re-lived moments I would've preferred to leave in the past. From my position in the interstices, I connected in with all of the diverse and disparate communities that I am blessed to belong to. I spoke to many friends and colleagues who suddenly found themselves on the frontlines, and I spent hours on coaching calls, helping leaders to navigate the greatest period of change and uncertainty that they'd ever faced. I listened deeply and tuned my attention, gradually coalescing fragments of ideas until, finally, I could see the patterns. Those patterns are presented in the framework you will find in this book.

It is a framework that distills the wisdom, learning, and insights developed from my own efforts of trying to shape meaningful and transformative change, as well as the many people I've had the honor to work alongside. But I don't want to prescribe a simple one-two-three process of how to create change. In fact, that kind of linear how-to thinking is contrary to the patterns themselves. And yet we are so conditioned to think in straight lines. To value answers over questions. To deem something's worth only if it can be summarized in a three-minute elevator pitch. Not having it presented that way is going to be uncomfortable, perhaps even frustrating. I get it. So to try to relieve some of your discomfort, I'll get uncomfortable with you—I haven't held back from being open and honest in sharing my failings and shortcomings from my own journey over the years. And despite the discomfort, I promise it's worth it.

I know what it's like to face seemingly insurmountable odds and feel powerless to make a difference. I know it can feel impossible. But in these pages, you will rediscover your sense of agency. You'll build your capability to engage with the world in a way that's effective and regenerative. You'll deepen your understanding of how and why change happens. And you'll find faith in your own ability to shape change. It is a deeply satisfying and joyful experience.

I also know that for many of us, the idea of changing the world can feel overwhelming, especially given the myriad struggles of day-to-day life. Take a deep breath and pause for a moment. You don't need to drop everything and take to the streets, nor do you need to go looking for new places or compelling issues.

The ideas presented in *The Weaver's Way* can be used to create change whoever, and wherever, you are. This book doesn't ask you to be a hero or a martyr. It simply asks you to show up for yourself and for others. To look around you and notice the abundance of opportunities for shaping change to make the world a better place. And to begin to do so.

For too long, mainstream messaging from the media, politicians, and corporations has tried to convince us that ordinary people will never change anything. I know that isn't true. I'm determined to ensure that the next generation knows it, and my wish is that you and I do it together.

But this is not just a wish. It is, I suppose, an existential necessity. I want to draw your attention to two important letters in this book's title. The *We*, in *The Weaver's Way*. That little word has a large role to play in this book. Indeed, in our future on this planet. So let's take a moment to talk about it. "We" is the magic that happens in the space between you and me. It's a word that implies complicity and seeks consent: I can extend a hand from me to you, but *me* does not become *we* until the invitation is accepted. There is magic in that moment, when we move from the individual to the collective. When *me* becomes *we* becomes *us* becomes *ours*. All of us, together, working for our collective future and wellbeing on this planet we call home.

This book is about shaping change through a framework that challenges old, ossified ways of thinking and acting, while shining a light on new ways of being and doing that reinforce a narrative of strength through interconnectedness. But it doesn't exist without you.

Because without you, there is no *we*. And without *we*, there are no Weavers.

And what of the Weavers? Who are they in this story?

Weavers is the name I give to those working to shape change. To solve problems through interconnectedness. Those who heal, support, and strengthen our social fabric. Who care for and mend the connective threads that bind us. Those who bring together movements and ideas, creating beauty and functionality in difference as well as similarity. People like you and me.

Deeply entrenched in the communities and places they serve, Weavers are better equipped to respond with flexibility and agility to rapidly changing or unexpected shifts in the ecosystem. They have a deep knowledge of the systems they're part of and are positioned to change and influence those systems. And perhaps most importantly of all: when the going gets tough, they aren't going anywhere.

THE WEAVER'S GUILD

guild: /gɪld/

Noun: *an association of people for mutual aid or the pursuit of a common goal*

Throughout *The Weaver's Way* I've incorporated real-life stories and examples from actual and metaphorical weavers. The purpose of this is twofold. First, it's to help illustrate how the principles of the framework apply in practice. But equally as important, it is to honor these Weavers, to lift up their voices, and to give their stories the place they deserve in our collective history. After all, it is their wisdom and experience that has made this book possible.

Interspersed throughout the following chapters are a handful of people whom I've had the pleasure to work with and walk alongside over the course of discovering my own Weaving story. Each of these people exemplifies some aspect of *The Weaver's Way* framework, and if there were such a thing as a Weaver's Guild, they would be in it. These names come from a much larger list of people whose stories I would be honored to share; however I've tried to intentionally select a small handful who I hope demonstrate the breadth and diversity of stories that *The Weaver's Way* makes possible.

In many ways there is an irony in trying to lift up individual Weavers to tell their story. As a Buddhist would say, it is like trying to capture water with a sieve. A Weaver, by nature, sees their work as part of a broader collective effort, and so highlighting just their contribution can feel uncomfortable or inauthentic. And so I want to express once again here my gratitude to them for saying yes to my invitation, and allowing me to share their stories.

I also want to emphasize that I don't share their stories so they can be placed up on a pedestal, to be exonerated in some history book of Great Weavers or made into heroes. No, these people walk among us. You will see in these small snapshots of their lives that they come from all walks of life and work in many different industries and sectors. But most importantly, what I hope you will see is that, with the deepest respect to them and their work, they are ordinary people, just like you and me. Everyday people who in their day-to-day lives are committed to going against the flow, to asking better questions, to working authentically and inclusively but most importantly, to taking responsibility for fellow human beings and translating it into actions to create a future we can all live with. Ordinary people doing extraordinary things, using Weaving as a means to shape change, call forth the future, and make it count.

CALLING ALL WEAVERS

For too long, the stories of change that we've been told have been dominated by heroes and saviors, steeped in the misguided mythology of singular achievement. Now is the time to celebrate the stories of Weavers.

Around the world, throughout the COVID-19 pandemic, people cried out in desperation to "get back to normal." Is that really what we want? "Normal never was," writes author and activist Sonya Renee

Taylor. "Our pre-corona existence was not normal, other than that we normalized greed, inequity, exhaustion, depletion, extraction, disconnection, confusion, rage, hoarding, hate and lack." Those words find resonance within me. "We should not long to return," she adds. "We are being given the opportunity to stitch a new garment. One that fits all of humanity and nature."

That includes you. This book is your invitation to become a Weaver.

My hope is this book helps to create a groundswell of people—Weavers—ready to engage in the world in a new way, and that together, we can begin building a society we can feel proud of. My hope is this book helps you, beloved Reader, to become more powerful and purposeful, knowing every step you take, every decision you make, you have the choice to make the world a softer, gentler place. In the words of Indian author and activist Arundhati Roy, "Another world is not only possible, she's on her way. Maybe many of us won't be here to greet her, but on a quiet day, if I listen very carefully, I can hear her breathing."[1]

The Weaver's Way is divided into three parts. Part I, "A Narrative for the Twenty-First Century," examines our stories about change. Chapter 1 explores how our stories influence the set of beliefs we hold about the world around us and our place in it and looks at how our existing stories lead us to develop self-limiting beliefs about who has the power, position, permission, and perspective to create change. Chapter 2 is about possibility, inviting you to start thinking about the kind of future you could begin to call forth if you embraced a different story about creating change. And Chapter 3 is about writing that story.

Part II of the book, "We, The Weavers," is much more practical, demonstrating how to apply this idea of a new story about change to the things that *you* want to change. It's about looking at what that new story needs to be so we can learn to shape change and make it count. If Part I gets you fired up about shaping change, then Part II will help you discover the right kinds of fuel to keep that fire burning in a *good* way. Fire, as I'm sure you know, can be constructive—illuminating, sustaining, and regenerating—or it can be destructive, burning and consuming all that lies in its path. So it is with change. As you'll discover in Part II, *how* you shape change is as important as the final result.

In Chapter 4 I introduce the idea of a framework for creating your new story of change called *The Weaver's Way*. I've created this framework from over a decade working with groups and individuals who arguably form some of the most marginalized in the world. They used this framework to create meaningful change despite some of the most difficult circumstances. I'm certain that if it worked for them, it can work for you.

In Chapter 5, I explain the components of this framework. In this chapter you'll also meet two people who are very special to me—Abigail and her mother, Loida. These conversations between Abigail, Loida, and myself—crossing generations, languages, culture, and worldviews—hold the precious seeds of wisdom at the heart of this work.

In Chapters 6 through 10 we continue to explore the building blocks of the framework. I show how you can put this framework into action with examples, stories, and tips. Interspersed throughout these chapters you'll also continue to meet members of the Weaver's Guild. I'm so excited for you to meet them and read their stories. These Weavers and their stories provide wonderful examples of how you can use *The Weaver's Way* framework to shape change, call forth the future, and make it count.

Chapters include worksheets or other interactive activities, exercises, and opportunities for reflection. This is for you if you're practically oriented. You don't have to do these exercises as you're reading the book. It might make sense to do it as you're reading to help to deepen your understanding. But you might discover things you want to return to days or even months after you've read the book. This is your journey, so do what works for you.

At the end of each chapter, you'll also find a bullet-point summary of the key takeaways. I find this helpful so I can lose myself in the narrative, but still be clear about where the book is heading at the end of each chapter. It can also be useful to keep as a reference as you begin your own journey of shaping change.

In Part III, Chapters 11 and 12, you'll see that we are surrounded by Weavers, and that being a Weaver is not about being a martyr. I'll also share a story that drives the point home that the power to change our own perspectives is in our hands.

Finally, I've provided a short further reading and resource section at the end of the book. That's where you should go if you want more information about any particular topic.

PART ONE
A NARRATIVE FOR THE TWENTY-FIRST CENTURY

CHAPTER 1
NOT JUST ANOTHER STORY

 History isn't what happened. It's who tells the story.

— DR. SALLY ROESCH WAGNER

I rested my head against the window of the bus, no longer alarmed by the fact that our ability to come to a stop seemed in no small part to rely on the ability of the *ayudante* (who couldn't be more than twelve years old) to swing out of the slowing vehicle and throw a couple of large pieces of timber under the front wheel as the bus gradually made its way to a halt.

Two women, unfazed by this seemingly risky means of stopping, waited patiently for the bus. They were dressed in the colorfully embroidered *güipiles* (blouses) and brightly colored *faldas* (skirts) that marked them as indigenous Maya. As the bus came to a stop, they passed the large and heavy-looking baskets they carried on their heads up to another young man who—despite treacherously high-speed maneuvering along the winding mountain roads—seemed to occupy a permanent position on the roof of the bus.

He swung the baskets up and stacked them among the others. The assortment of fruit and vegetables and brightly colored textiles and livestock (the latter being what earned Guatemala's *chicken buses* their fame among tourists) reminded me of the overly ambitious hats my sisters and I would make for the annual Easter Hat Parade at Jiggi Valley Primary School when we were children.

Inside the bus, despite the fact I'm only 5'4" (on a good day), my knees already pressed uncomfortably into the seat in front. When the old U.S. school buses make their way down to Guatemala, the seats are always removed and reinstalled closer together, a routine part of the chicken bus makeover, in an effort to fit in as many passengers as possible. I tried to make myself even smaller as my seat (originally designed to fit two young school children) was ambitiously offered up to accommodate the women who had just gotten on. I closed my eyes briefly and imagined myself curled up at home on our antique family sofa, all padding, curves, and embroidery. The enforced proximity was a welcome counterpoint to the loneliness I felt inside. The bus roared off once again, and my gaze drifted back to the world outside.

A few months earlier my life had been abruptly upended, and I'd rapidly thrown together this *vacation*—a desperate attempt to escape the constant reminders of loss and betrayal that threatened to overwhelm me back home. Just six months earlier I'd felt life couldn't get any better: career on track, an amazing relationship, feeling confident to start home ownership with the man I thought I'd spend the rest of my life with. *How did I get it so wrong?*

I stared out the window at the villages rushing by, then up to the horizon where the first rays of sun were just rising above the impressive volcano-dotted skyline. I thought back to the sunrises I would watch each morning over Sydney harbor from my desk on the top floor of our corporate headquarters. My desk, hurriedly stripped bare of the smiling, happy couple photos right before I left. Did it feel as vulnerable and exposed as I did? Well, this was as far away as I could get from those painful memories.

Little did I realize, it was just the beginning. The beginning of a journey that has been so life-changing, so transformative, that I've no other option but to look back on those painful memories with grace and gratitude.

Growing up, my sisters and I were raised on a solid diet of climate change doom and gloom, and anti-capitalist thinking. Not exactly *preppers*, our parents nevertheless had decided before we were born to leave the seductive lure of the big city and become self-sufficient: growing food, raising livestock, and generally living off the land. By the time three young children came around, my parents had reevaluated their priorities and decided to embrace some of the modern conveniences like an indoor flush toilet and supermarkets, but the *alternative* lifestyle was still a defining part of my character.

Before I'd even reached my teens, I was an active member of the local youth environment group, speaking at anti-mining protests, organizing events, and raising money for different environmental causes. A much less prominent but no less passionate Greta Thunburg from another era, I even wrote a letter or two to David Attenborough (alas, it was pre-podcast era). From a young age, I was determined to build a career working in the then-nascent field of sustainability, although I'd decided—contrary to my parents' approach—that I needed to be in the belly of the beast.

And I'd made it. I'd studied engineering, got my first job with a consulting firm, and by twenty-five I'd secured a sustainability focused role with Australia's largest investment bank. Creating change from the inside, I would tell myself. Or was I?

As I stared out the window of the bus, I caught a glimpse of trash-strewn streets, barefoot, runny-nosed children playing at the edges of smoking garbage dumps, and ramshackle huts cobbled together from concrete blocks and sheets of corrugated iron. This wasn't my first time visiting a developing country, but something about the circumstances of this particular trip made it different. Perhaps it was my own vulnerability, broken open as I was, that allowed the truth of what I was seeing to really hit home.

Whatever the reason, with each bone-shuddering jolt over one of the hundreds of *topes* (homemade speed bumps of varying shapes and sizes), I felt an equally jarring mental shudder as the ignorance and innocence of youth was replaced with the kind of painful realization that marks so many of the milestones into adulthood.

On countless occasions prior to this journey, I'd spoken passionately about the injustices of climate change—how the poorest and most vulnerable would be the first and hardest hit. It was something I knew intellectually, but as I was soon to discover, there is knowing, and there is *knowing*—the kind of visceral, bone-deep knowing from which there is no turning back.

After my vacation, I returned to Sydney. I was determined to forget about my sorrow and focus on my career. But, as I was soon to discover, I'd left behind one heartbreak for another. What I'd witnessed in Guatemala had led me to the inevitable conclusion that the idea of sustainability on which I'd built my identity was a sham: truly a rich man's luxury and a poor man's obligation. Did I really think I was creating change, or had I just found a comfortable way to assuage my consciousness, while disguising an inconvenient truth with a reassuring lie?

Over the next two years, I spent more time in Guatemala than back in Sydney. I was searching for a way I could create change that didn't just pay lip service to an idea, but that was truly transformative. A way that felt more authentic and aligned with my beliefs and values.

But I was unsuccessful. And so my restlessness grew until one day, I decided to take my search one step further. I quit my job, purchased a one-way ticket to San Francisco, found a used car for under $1,000, and pointed it toward Central America. I'd no greater plans than to begin a journey of listening to myself, to the people around me, and to the planet I deeply loved and cared for. I was about to turn twenty-seven.

Almost 6,000 kilometers later, approximately two hours northeast of El Salvador's capital, I ended one journey and began another. I'd made my way to El Papaturro, a tiny rural village that had been settled in 1992 by refugees returning after the civil war. I'd heard there was a community-based agro-ecology farm in the area, and I was interested in visiting to learn more about what they were doing. I parked my car on the side of the road. There was no sign of civilization apart from a hand-painted wooden sign welcoming people to the center and a small dirt path wandering up the hill away from the road. I started along, calling out as I did so. After a minute or so my questioning "holas" were met with an answering "Ho!" and I saw a young man wearing a long-sleeved button-up shirt, a pair of old jeans, and a big smile, waving at me with a cob of corn. "It's hot down there," he called out. "Come up to the shed." The shed, it turned out, consisted of an area about twelve square meters, covered in a few old sheets of tin. It wasn't much, but it felt good to get out of the sweltering sun.

The contents of the shed were as simple as the structure itself: a large sheet of black plastic piled high with dried cobs of corn of various shades of red, yellow, and orange and a couple of overturned wooden packing crates, which, looking at my new host, apparently served as seats. Antonio gestured at one of the crates with his corn cob—an invitation to sit down I assumed—and explained that this was *criollo* (heirloom) corn and that he was in the process of shelling—removing the kernels to save for the next crop. Briefly explaining who I was and my purpose in visiting the farm, I asked Antonio if I could help while I asked him a few questions.

He readily agreed, although it turned out to be Antonio who did most of the asking. He peppered me with questions, first about renewable energy and appropriate technology, then switching to the science of climate change and the impacts it might have on El Salvador and neighboring countries. It wasn't long before I had picked up my own dried cob of corn, which I began using to draw sketches and diagrams into the baked brown earth at our feet as I responded to Antonio's inquiring mind. I answered where I could and told him I'd get back to him where I couldn't. In between explanations and drawings I eventually picked up the rhythm, if not the skill, of shelling, and our activities carried us well into late afternoon until the rumbling of our empty stomachs finally managed to win out over our enthusiasm for sharing ideas.

Noticing how late in the day it was, I reluctantly announced that I should probably head into town to find something to eat and somewhere to sleep for the night. With a huge smile, Antonio offered to introduce me to El Salvador's famous *pupusas* if, in exchange, I would help him design a biodigester (a low-cost technology that would convert the dung from his family's cows into gas they could use for cooking). Now it was my turn to readily agree.

And so it was that there, beneath the hot and sweaty sun, two kinds of seeds were collected. The corn seeds for next year's harvest, and the seeds of a new friendship and partnership that would drastically impact the course of both of our lives, and thousands of other young people as well.

That evening, lying awake in the room I'd rented from a family known to Antonio, it dawned on me. So many of the projects and initiatives I'd come across when I'd been searching for a way to get involved centered around implementing the ideas and solutions of outsiders. I thought about that day with Antonio and all we'd discussed. Yes, by virtue of my background and upbringing I had access to certain information and resources, but the relevance paled in comparison to the wealth of contextual knowledge Antonio brought to the table.

He knew *this* place and *these* people. The problems we'd been discussing were part of his day-to-day reality. He knew best what was happening, so why would it be anyone *but* Antonio who would drive the solution? I'd found what I'd come here to do. I look now at the note that I wrote to myself before I fell asleep that evening: *all that I have, all that I am, to help Antonio be all he dreams to be.*

I'd found a job working night shifts at a bar in a tourist town in Guatemala, so that I could spend my days continuing my journey of listening and learning. I started visiting Antonio's community for two to three days at a time on my days off. We built a biodigester. We worked on making a permaculture garden and organic fertilizer. He proudly walked me through the meandering dirt paths of his community to show me the trash cans their youth group had placed to stop people littering, and the hand-painted wooden signs reminding people to Protect the Environment, Don't Litter, and Love Mother Nature.

We organized workshops to run with his environmental group and more activities for cleaning up the community and planting trees around the two springs that provided the community's water. After a few months working together, Antonio told me about a group of youth in a neighboring community. They had come to El Papaturro and seen everything Antonio and his group of young activists were doing, and they wanted to learn more. Would I be willing to accompany Antonio and his group for a visit?

The answer, of course, was yes. The energy, ideas, and enthusiasm of these young people—their willingness to try to address the problems they saw around them—was a source of inspiration to me. I, in turn, responded with whatever tools, resources, training, or other support they asked for. Word spread, ad-hoc workshops turned into training programs and retreats for young leaders wanting to make a difference in their communities, and before we knew it, this grassroots youth-led organizing and activism had turned into a movement of young changemakers and a UNESCO award-winning organization we named SERES. The word ser or sere (plural seres) has meaning in a number of languages. The Latin etymology of the word is both "I plant" as well as "I weave." In Spanish, it means "to be." While in English, the word seres comes from ecology and refers to a natural succession of communities in an ecosystem, succeeding one another to the point when a steady state, or balance, is achieved. That, of course, was much too complicated for most people, so we ended up just making it an acronym: social equity, resilience, and ecological sustainability. I served as the executive director of SERES for ten years.

Since that fateful first meeting with Antonio, as executive director of SERES and later as a coach, consultant, and mentor, I have remained passionately dedicated to supporting individuals and organizations to shape change. Specifically, change designed to help address some of the most urgent challenges of our time: issues such as climate change, social inequality, environmental degradation, poverty, and structural racism.

Throughout it all, the question that originally caused me to head south from San Francisco in a written-off Subaru has not changed. In fact, it has become the question that drives what I now consider my life's work: to understand what it takes to create meaningful change at a scale and pace that will help bring about the kind of future we can all live with.

CHANGING THE LEADERS OR LEADING THE CHANGE

When I first started working on this book, Kathy, a dear friend and my early editor, asked me, "So, is this a book about creating change, or a book about leadership?" For me, these two concepts are so deeply woven together I find it difficult to talk about one without bringing in the other. This book, I explained to Kathy, is a call to action, an invitation to engage in a meaningful way, in service to a better world. But still, a lot of questions remained.

Was it for people who were active in creating change, or instrumental in leading it? Already making change happen, or wanting to get started? And what about the size of the change? Was this as relevant for someone wanting to create change in their child's cafeteria lunch menu as it was for those who wanted to change the way their organization operated? Was I targeting the *formal* change sector (e.g., development, humanitarian aid, and social innovation), or everyday people? The answer was clear to me (tick all of the above), but not yet as clear to those helping me bring this labor of love to life.

Perhaps it was so hard to define because of the paradoxical, immutable nature of change itself. As they say, the only constant is change, as inevitable as death and taxes. It was while reflecting on the purpose of this book that I stumbled across the work of Octavia Butler, the first Black American woman to gain popularity and critical acclaim as a major science fiction writer. My first exposure to Butler's literary talent was through the Earthseed series, which, although written almost two decades before I first read her work, outlines an unnervingly prescient vision of an alternative future that foresaw many aspects of life today.

The central theme of the book is the idea that change is universal. The only lasting truth. And that we cannot create change without ourselves being changed. That has certainly been true of my own experience. But what was the story that I needed to tell?

The words were there, on the lips of Butler's fifteen-year-old Black protagonist. "Shape change" she urges from that fictional dystopian future where humankind has failed to do just that. *Shape change.*

Because the truth is that large or small, each and every one of us is involved in creating change every day. The question lies in whether or not we do so intentionally, in ways that are aligned with our values and aspirations for the kind of world we wish to live in. Or do we do it accidentally, as victims to the inertia of *the way things are*? Are we doing the hard work of turning to face the difficult truths of a world out of balance or do we avert our gaze, turning away from an opportunity to create the change we know needs to happen? It's a choice we make a hundred times over, every single day. Most of us strive for the former yet are often guilty of the latter. These feelings of guilt combine with our feelings of helplessness into anger and frustration at the status quo. We complain, but we don't change.

Living and working on three continents, I've realized two things: most people, when invited to reflect on the state of the world around them, agree passionately that change is required, and similarly, most believe there is very little they can do to create, shape, or influence change. And perhaps most surprising of all—the further I step away from the frontlines, away from the impoverished and marginalized communities I've considered home for the last fifteen years, the stronger that feeling of powerlessness becomes. Even, it seems, amongst the world's most powerful.

THE POWERLESS POWERFUL

Some years back, I was invited to participate in an executive leadership seminar, which the organizer's website said was "to support and stimulate leaders in their commitment to create better societies." The other participants were primarily either private-sector executives representing Central America's largest multinational businesses or members from the region's rich and powerful elite families. It was, truly, a selection of the most highly influential leaders in the region.

It was also, as I gradually came to realize, a group of people whose intuitions and sympathies were limited by the circumstances of their birth.

Not surprisingly I, being someone who had only recently discovered that *Coach* represented something other than the class of ticket I traveled on, felt distinctly out of place. When we gathered in the seminar room at our first meeting, I found the sheer amount of wealth and power seated in that circle hard to comprehend.

I thought about the young leaders we were working with in SERES. With little more than grit and determination, these young people were managing to create impact not just at a local level, but increasingly at municipal and state levels as well. Imagine what they could do with the kind of resources in this room at their disposal, I thought. Surely if anyone wanted to create change, to tackle "the foremost societal challenges of our times" (as this program claimed to do), any one member of this group could do so with a click of their fingers. But as we sat through the seminars, discussing the challenges and promises of leadership and debating Plato and Socrates and other great thinkers throughout the ages, it dawned on me that I was sadly mistaken.

Much to my surprise, as we gradually came to a consensus that change was, indeed, needed, those very same questions about who has the power, the permission, the position and the perspective to create change emerged. There they hung in the air between us, uncomfortably pregnant pauses in what was otherwise a robust dialogue.

And rather than being met with a resounding "we do," they seemed to provoke the same kind of doubt and uncertainty that felt just as insurmountable here, in this gilded seminar room, as it felt out there in the real world.

"You do," I wanted to shout in despair. "Can't you see?"

Later that evening I sat alone in my room, feeling demoralized. When I had agreed to participate in this program, I had high hopes about the kinds of changes it could mean for the region. I dreamed of being able to bring voices from the margins to the center and moving resources from the center to the margins: bridging the decades-old divide between the wealthy and the poor with a common vision and commitment to collective action that would help address the rapidly growing list of problems the region was facing.

But it wasn't to be. I was crushed with an overwhelming disappointment in myself and my abilities, like a physical weight on my chest that made it difficult to breathe. Names, faces, and stories of SERES youth who I had been with just the week before scrolled through my mind.

Wilson, trying to stop corruption and make local council dealings more transparent.

Fatima, running a campaign to stop violence against women.

Ludwin, putting his life on the line to stop the multinational mining company from taking their lands and poisoning their rivers.

Dedicated and passionate young people working tirelessly to give their country a different future while I sat here in a five-star resort, unable to get them the support they needed and deserved.

Ping. The screen of my phone lit up to break the darkness and my equally dark ruminations. It was my friend, Julie.

Julie: Hi [smiley face emoji]. How's the big leadership seminar going? [Excited emoji, strong emoji, celebration emoji].

Me: Not great [sad face emoji].

Julie: Oh no [cry emoji]. What's happened?

Me: Nothing...that's the point.

Through the modern-day messaging miracle of truncated

sentences and ideograms, I manage to release all the frustration and disappointment I was feeling. "I just don't get it. If it isn't their job, then just whose job IS it?"

"Oh," wrote Julie, "you mean like that leadership story 'Whose Job Is It Anyway?' that everyone uses in team building workshops?"

I opened a web browser on my phone and typed it in, and there it was.

"Here's a little story about changing the world," read the article, which went something like this:

There are four people named Everybody, Somebody, Anybody, and Nobody. There was an important job to be done, and Everybody was sure that Somebody would do it. Anybody could have done it, but Nobody did it. Somebody got angry about that, because it was Everybody's job. Everybody thought Anybody could do it, but Nobody realized that Everybody wouldn't do it. It ended up that Everybody blamed Somebody when Nobody did what Anybody could have.

I don't know how accurate it is to say that this is a story about changing the world. But what I can say for certain is that this story changed *my* world.

WHOSE JOB IS IT, ANYWAY?

Over the years of supporting people to take action on the issues that most concern them, I've come to realize that the reasons for *not* taking action generally fall into one of four categories: power, permission, position, perspective.

"I don't have any power..."

"*They* wouldn't talk/listen to *me*..."

"I'm not in a leadership position..."

"I don't know if what I want to do is right/will work..."

"Why do I have to do it? What about him/her/them?"

"It's [insert position]'s job!"

If I was someone else—those fears and doubts seemed to say—or *something* else, then I could do it.

So who do you have to be, I would ask, to begin taking action on this thing that is so clearly important to you?

That night after the leadership seminar, I lay awake thinking. "Whose Job Is It, Anyway?" was another way of asking that same question. It didn't seem to matter whether I was speaking with the most downtrodden members of society or its wealthy and elite. It was still a question of who had the power, permission, position, and perspective to shape change. How had this become such a pervasive problem?

My thoughts returned to the "Whose Job Is It Anyway?" anecdote. It's a story commonly used to emphasize the importance of leadership and taking accountability and responsibility. But really, what kind of story names its characters Everybody, Somebody, Anybody and Nobody? I'd rather be the Big Bad Wolf—at least he had flair! Those characters weren't inspiring; I didn't identify with any of them.

But what of our other stories? What role did they play in influencing how we thought about shaping change?

I had always thought about story time as something I did with my nieces and nephew, stopping when they became old enough to put themselves to bed. But the reality is story time never ends. Stories are instrumental in shaping the way we see the world, the way we think about solutions, and the way we see ourselves as actors within those solutions. So could it be that our stories about whose job it is to create change are responsible for all of the self-limiting beliefs I kept encountering again and again?

The simple answer is yes.

As I began examining the different stories we have around creating change, I came to see how the protagonists of those stories—"leaders" we call them—could be just as uninspiring as our other characters: Everybody, Somebody, Anybody, and Nobody. If I was going to be inspired by those stories, I needed a different protagonist. A new kind of leader.

WILBUR, MY KIND OF LEADER

Wilbur is a young man I first met many years ago, when I was in El Salvador with Antonio. Wilbur is from the small rural community of Celina Ramos, population approximately 150. Back in 2014 Celina Ramos was just one of hundreds of rural towns and villages across the tiny country that would be rapidly overtaken by a growing epidemic of violence after the disintegration of a government-brokered truce agreement between rival gangs.

What ensued in the months and years after was a deadly battle of power that gave El Salvador the unwelcome reputation of being the deadliest country outside of a war zone. With the state on one side and various gang factions on the other, young men like Wilbur became currency, their lives spent thoughtlessly in indiscriminate killings by state-supported troops or violently recruited into the deadly gangs. Faced with a terrifying and seemingly hopeless situation, thousands of children and young adults made the difficult and dangerous decision to leave their country and migrate north to the United States.

But not Wilbur.

SERES had been working in and around Celina Ramos since about 2010. Our approach was to work with groups of young people from a particular area, providing workshops, training, and resources to support them as they began to take action in their communities. Our first step together was to dream: helping participants to visualize the kind of future they wanted for themselves and their community. Then, they'd use that vision to define the kinds of changes that had to take place: improved stewardship of the community's resources, leadership roles for women, safer streets. Next, we would discuss what kinds of things needed to shift in order to create those changes, and finally we asked: what are *you* going to do to achieve them?

It might seem unfair or unreasonable to place this responsibility onto Wilbur's and others' young shoulders, but this framing was an important part of our approach. Because this was the beginning of a new story—*their* story—in which, instead of being the victims, they were to be the protagonists—the leaders.

But even as we did this, we quickly came to realize that rewriting the story wasn't as simple as changing who got to play the main characters. We were calling up young people to be leaders when the generation that preceded them still held the physical and emotional scars of decades of civil war. For many, the idea of being a leader was anathema, the mantle of leadership imbued with the stench of violence, corruption, and betrayal.

While I know many societies—especially in the West—haven't experienced this same level of civil unrest and political upheaval, it still seems that for more and more of us, our traditional business and political leaders are busy pursuing goals that are ever more distant from the needs and desires of those whom they purport to be leading. For the purposes of this book, let's call them big "L" Leaders (as distinct from leaders).

So who are these so-called Leaders? These Leaders are the winners of a game so many of us are playing without ever realizing. A Game whose unwritten rules are the accumulation of power and the amassing of resources. The better you are at the Game, the further you rise to the top. Then—and this part is crucial—since we tend to think of Leaders as those who sit in positions of power, we attribute the characteristics of leader*ship* to those at the top. And this subconscious attribution has big implications when it comes to our self-limiting beliefs about who has the power, permission, position, and perspective to create change. Or to put it another way, when it comes to whose job it is to shape change.

When we cannot identify with the characters within a story, we either strive to emulate that which we are not, or we disconnect and turn away. The first gives rise to feelings of unworthiness and inauthenticity; we are imposters waiting to be discovered. The second creates a sense of powerlessness, resulting in apathy and disinterest. To these so-called Leaders we endow the power, position, permission, and perspective, the *privilege*, of shaping change, while at the same time denying ourselves the ability to take action on the things that are most important to us. It is the great malaise of the twenty-first century. So what is the prognosis, and—perhaps more importantly—is there a cure? The answer is yes. But before we examine ways we might end this affliction, let's take a moment to examine the risks of inaction.

PROGNOSIS

So what is the prognosis for this chronic condition that seems to plague so many of us? To understand one possible scenario, I want to take a moment and introduce you to the group of women who inspired the name for this book—Indigenous Maya women from across Guatemala's highlands.

Visit any rural community in Guatemala's highlands, and you're bound to come across an indigenous woman weaving. You'll most likely find her kneeling on the floor or sitting on a low three-legged stool with her loom (the device used for weaving) stretched out in front. Chances are she'll be weaving on what is known as a backstrap loom, so named for the strap that winds around her back. The other end is hooked onto a post or tied to a tree, and the complex, colorful confusion of threads and sticks that form the warp stretches out in front of her.

Throughout the country and increasingly in wealthy nations around the world, you will see evidence of her handicraft. From the traditional dress of brightly colored, loose-fitting tunics and long, heavy skirts of the women I shared a bus ride with to everyday objects like napkins and placemats and even strutting down the runway as part of a designer fashion brand's latest look.

These Maya women and their vibrant, colorful textiles and indigenous costume are one of the most iconic images of Guatemala. They represent over 2,000 years of oral history passed down through generations of women, in a quiet resistance against the hegemonic forces first of colonization and, later, free market capitalism. The omnipresence of these textiles in so many aspects of everyday

Guatemalan life speaks to the strength and resilience of these women weavers, but these qualities are rarely spoken of.

The shadow side to this rich cultural history is that Guatemala's indigenous women are one of the most marginalized demographics in the country. A sobering report released by UNICEF[1] in 2018 revealed that despite many efforts over the preceding ten years, very little progress had been made toward advancing the plight of indigenous women and girls. The report could easily be summarized by the following bleak conclusion: to be born indigenous and female in Guatemala is an almost guaranteed future of illness, illiteracy, and violence.

Here we have a paradox, two seemingly incongruous realities. How could it be that these women, bastions of the country's rich bio-cultural heritage and undoubtedly one of the most recognized cultural icons outside of Guatemala, could be so undervalued by the very same society?

Is it really true, as the report says, that these women, part of an intergenerational effort that has kept tradition and culture alive despite centuries of violence in the form of invasion, colonization, and civil war, really are "the most vulnerable?" It begs the question, what are they vulnerable to?

Perhaps, as Palestinian poet Mourid Barghouti would argue, they are vulnerable to the storyteller. As he writes in his book, *I Saw Ramallah* "It is easy to blur the truth with a simple linguistic trick: start your story from 'Secondly.' ...Start your story with 'Secondly,' and the world will be turned upside-down. Start your story with 'Secondly,' and the arrows of the Red Indians are the original criminals and the guns of the white men are entirely the victims. It is enough to start with 'Secondly,' for the anger of the black man against the white to be barbarous. Start with 'Secondly,' and Gandhi becomes responsible for the tragedies of the British."[2] What Barghouti is referring to is a tendency in our storytelling to neglect to talk about what happened first.

The story told about the vulnerability of Guatemala's indigenous women is a story that starts with secondly. It is not the only one. So often, when we encounter people and places that have been degraded, discarded, and marginalized, the stories we use to make sense of what we are seeing start with secondly.

What we don't seem to realize is that we are all a part of the same story, and it is all being told the same way. It may be that we haven't yet reached the chapter where we ourselves are the most vulnerable, but I think of the families and friends that I worked beside after the Guatemalan eruption and Lismore's floods and can't help but wonder —how much longer until my own story starts with secondly? Wherever in the world you may be right now, we can no longer afford the luxury of feeling powerless. It's time for change, starting with our stories about change itself. But before we can do that, we need to dig a little deeper.

SUMMARY

- The stories we tell have a powerful effect on our lives. They influence the set of beliefs we hold about the world and our place in it, leading us to develop self-limiting beliefs about who has the power, position, permission, and perspective to create change.
- As a society, we've given away the privilege of shaping change, allowing power to be concentrated in the hands of a few, whose abilities and motives are often questionable and who do not always represent the values and interests of the people and society they are supposed to be serving.
- We can reclaim our ability to shape change by rewriting our stories and creating new identities that embrace a new way of leading and leadership.

EXERCISES

1. WHAT'S HOLDING YOU BACK?

Think about the situations in your day-to-day life of things that you wish could be different but you feel unable to change. They could be things you see that frustrate or upset you; they could be relationships you find challenging, or some other set of personal circumstances. For each of the examples you come up with, write down the source of the blockage: power, position, permission, or perspective.

2. WHO DO YOU CHOOSE TO BE?

Choose one of the examples from the previous exercise and ask yourself, who would I have to be to be able to change this situation?

Write it down then read back over what you have written. Does this person have more power (from where?), a different position (in what?), permission (from whom?), a different perspective (how/why?) What insights does this give you about your own story and any self-limiting beliefs it may hold?

These two exercises are designed to help you uncover the stories you're telling about yourself. Neither power, position, permission nor perspective are immutable. They can all be changed, often easier than we think. But the first step in doing so is acknowledging the structures that keep them in place—the stories we tell about ourselves and each other!

CHAPTER 2

THE GAMES WE PLAY

Let us not pray to be sheltered from dangers but to be fearless when facing them.

— RABINDRANATH TAGORE

Stories, and the characters they contain, are one of the fundamental ways that we as human beings organize our understanding of the world. They shape our identities and help us make sense of the world and our role in it. These stories are then influenced and informed by our context, which provides greater meaning and nuance.

Take, for example, my identity as an aunt. What that means depends if I'm an aunt with my immediate family in Australia, an aunty among Australian First Nations people, a tía in Guatemala, or a zia in Italy. Different cultural norms and values govern the behaviors that are expected of that role, and they can change depending on where I am and who I'm relating to.

Underlying all of this are paradigms. Paradigms are the basic building blocks that control how we see the world. They are like the foundations, if you will, on which our stories and narratives are built. These paradigms are handed to us often without realizing, from influences such as our parents or guardians, our religion, our education system, our community, and the society in which we are raised. They shape our beliefs (how we explain how the world works) and our values (what we deem is worthy/good/attractive, or unworthy/bad/distasteful). Our paradigms are deeply embedded in our sense of self and our place in the world, so ingrained into our thinking and behavior that they are often invisible, even while influencing the choices and actions we make every day.

Most of the time the influence of these paradigms is subtle—guiding our actions and decisions in ways we are not even aware of. But subtlety should not be mistaken for softness. Because when you do come up against your own paradigms, even unknowingly, the impact can be world-shattering.

A TALE OF TWO TALES

For the ten years I was working full-time with SERES, I traveled back and forth between Central America, Australia, and the United States, raising awareness and looking for funding to support our work. Much of what I did during this time was made possible by the generosity of others. I traveled between cities because people donated their frequent flyer miles and airline points for flights. My wardrobe was filled with the pre-loved clothes of friends and family who would put aside a bag of hand-me-downs ahead of my next visit. I built community in dozens of towns as people opened their homes and gave me somewhere to rest and work. And, ultimately, the work of our organization was sustained through the generosity and good faith of people who dug into their own pockets to give to our cause.

As I found my way in this strange new world, I began to develop an acute appreciation that my life was grounded firmly in what I began to call the Gift Economy[1].

The Gift Economy told a beautiful story about money and

economics that was significantly different than the one I had been raised with. In this story, I had an important role to play: accepting the generosity of people, organizations, and institutions and transforming that into a fight for justice for people and the planet. It was a story in which I measured my success by the positive change we created together through SERES, and I was proud of the part I played.

In contrast, the story I was raised with took its cues from the meritocracy myth: study hard, work hard, and earn your way by working toward upward social mobility. I was born into a family without a lot of financial resources, so this social mobility was important. My worth would be proven by achieving financial success and independence, marked by ever-larger paychecks and a series of titles that reflected my climb up the corporate ladder.

When I allowed myself to fully embrace the story of the Gift Economy I felt powerful and successful, confident in my decision to leave the safety and security of my corporate career back in Sydney. But when the mainstream narrative took hold, as it normally did when visiting Australia or the USA, I would lie awake at night, anxious. I didn't have a house, a car, or savings. I wasn't putting money away into a retirement fund, I wasn't building my equity. I didn't have enough, therefore I wasn't enough.

I would drag myself out of bed in the morning, exhausted and demoralized. The support of friends and family was no longer a celebration of reciprocity and generosity but simply charity. I was poor, and I was a failure. Back and forth I swung between these two different stories, each one having vastly different impacts in terms of both how I saw myself as well as my work.

On reflection, however, "swinging" is perhaps not the best way to describe it. When I think of swinging, I imagine a gentle movement. A light flirtation with gravity. But moving between these two tales was much more violent. Each time this took hold of me, I felt the physical effects of an existential cognitive dissonance as I was thrown back and forth between two very different sets of values and beliefs. I was caught between these two paradigms: one that empowered and uplifted, the other that disempowered and demoralized. The first reflected the values and beliefs I wanted to live by. But the second? I was shocked by how pervasive and powerful this other story of "success" was: Where did it come from, and how could it have such a strong hold over me?

Not only had I just discovered the Game, I'd also discovered that I was an unwitting player. In how many other ways, I wondered, might I still be participating in the Game—mindlessly playing out a story that was handed to me without even realizing it?

Too many, it turned out.

But that wasn't the most troubling part. Even more disturbing to discover was that I wasn't just a hapless player of the Game. I was also an instigator.

THE FOUNDER FALLACY

When Antonio and I started working together, we never dreamt of building an organization, much less having the kind of reach and impact that SERES does today. It was, quite simply, two friends in their twenties who were caught up in the contagious energy and joy of seeing real change happen, right before our eyes.

As we continued to work with more and more young people, there was a natural evolution to build the infrastructure and resources to support it. Fundraising became increasingly important, the responsibility of which fell largely on my shoulders, primarily because it required a proficiency in English and an ability to travel freely and easily to countries in the global north like the United States and Canada. I started writing an increasing number of grant applications, not even realizing the very questions I was answering over and over again were influencing the evolution of our fledgling organization.

One of the most troubling of those questions was the one that asked how our solution was scalable. I always felt this question was at odds with the way we worked, which relied on relationships, contextual knowledge, and the drive and determination of local leaders. And yet the ones who controlled the funding insisted that the only successful solutions were those that could be scaled.

As I fumbled my way through the answers, the doubt began to creep in. Perhaps what we were doing wasn't really worthy, if we were not able to double our growth year-on-year. Or perhaps it was just that I didn't have the vision or ability to dream big enough.

Ironically, those feelings of doubt and inadequacy became particularly pervasive after we were awarded the inaugural UNESCO-Japan prize for Education for Sustainable Development in 2015. Imposter syndrome started to creep in, and I was constantly afraid we would suddenly be exposed as unworthy of such exalted recognition.

We were approached by multiple organizations and institutions that all wanted to take what we were doing and "scale it up." One such institution even flew me, along with a handful of other practitioners doing similarly transformative change work, to India. They put us up in an old raja's palace that had been converted into a luxury hotel, and we spent the week in workshops where we would "share our best practices." We were told they would take these best practices to develop an online training program that would reach millions of young people around the world.

My instinct told me it couldn't be done, that in the drive for efficiency and impact *en masse*, it would sacrifice the relationships and cultural nuances that were an essential part of making what we did transformational. At the same time my inner critic dragged me down for my inability to think big.

I thought about the kind of self-made, entrepreneurial champions who were often lauded as the heroes of creating change. Those with highly scalable solutions such as a new technology bringing drinking water to millions, or a fintech app that would help the poor across entire continents participate in banking. They were the real changemakers, and we needed to be more like them. Returning from that trip to India, I pushed myself hard to follow that model.

I began applying for different fellowships and programs for changemakers and taking courses for social entrepreneurship, challenging myself to follow the Leaders and to think more entrepreneurially. I focused my attention on driving down overhead, becoming more efficient, and developing metrics for monitoring and evaluating everything we did. And, of course, the pursuit of the entrepreneur's holy grail: scale!

Some time after this Antonio and I were at a small community near Puerto La Libertad in El Salvador. After a three-day workshop with local youth, the participants would hold a community forum about how climate change would impact their beachside town and share their ideas for taking action. Local leaders, elected officials, and parents were all invited to attend and stay for lunch.

As I helped in the last-minute preparations, the cook approached me. She explained that one of the facility security guards had been watching the youth working on their initiatives over the three days. He was curious to learn more and had asked her if he could attend the forum.

"No, it's not possible," I told her, hardly stopping to think. "We don't have enough food. We've budgeted for twenty-five guests, and that's all we can afford."

She nodded and walked away, but about ten minutes later, Antonio found me. It was one of the few times he has ever looked angry with me, and I stopped what I was doing and asked him what was wrong.

"Did you turn the security guard away?" he asked.

"Yes," I told him.

"He's a member of this community," he responded. "He should be there if he wants to be."

"You told me to budget for twenty-five guests," I shot back. That's what I did. We don't have enough food."

There was reproach in Antonio's eyes as he looked at me. "Where we come from, we always have enough to feed a guest."

I myself had been generously fed enough times out in the communities, in humble homes, often with dirt or concrete floors and wide gaps in timber-slatted walls, to feel the sting of Antonio's rebuke.

It was enough to at least make me apologize, but overall it wasn't sufficient to shift me from my trajectory.

This was just one of many small but significant mistakes I made during this time that in hindsight make me cringe. But back then I was determined to succeed. I'd been learning all I could about how to create change, and it all pointed to the fact that Antonio and I'd been doing it wrong.

But not anymore.

The changes I'd been implementing were finally working. I had my elevator pitch down to three minutes and was getting the opportunity to share it with more and more foundations. And those foundations were funding us to expand our programs to new and different areas where we had never been before. Not only that but I'd also (finally) made my way into what I jokingly referred to as the Funders and Founders Club. My calendar became full of conferences, networking events and happy hours. It was the social circle that I aspired to! Social entrepreneurs, start-up founders, foundation representatives and investors, all working for social impact.

Shortly after that community forum, I found myself at one of those events. The two settings couldn't have been more different. Gone were the fifty or so people crammed together on plastic chairs, sweating under the hot tropical sun beating down relentlessly on the tin roof.

Instead, well-dressed people wandered in small groups past beautifully lit water features or sat on couches scattered across the manicured lawn, sipping cocktails. The piles of steaming pupusas I had meticulously budgeted for (exactly two per person) were replaced by waiters bearing endless trays of drinks and canapés. A four-piece string quartet stood in lieu of the nonstop sound of merengue that was the unavoidable soundtrack in any rural community in El Salvador. I was getting increasingly used to this extreme code-switching but still, it felt surreal.

Casting around for familiar faces, I followed the pull of the crowd into the house to an inner courtyard, where beautiful emerald vine flowers hung delicately above our heads. Our host, a Guatemalan businessman, was preparing to share a few words of welcome. Catering to the crowd, he began by sharing a story about an event he'd just attended for a successful and well-known Guatemalan social enterprise.

The enterprise sells handmade bracelets and other handicrafts made by indigenous Guatemalan women, most of whom survive on less than two dollars a day. They'd just launched a new product line, and the event, held in one of the highland villages that was home to a group of women weavers, was to celebrate this milestone.

Public infrastructure investment in Guatemala's rural areas, which is about eighty percent indigenous, is amongst the lowest in Latin America. One of the many consequences of this is long, arduous, and often dangerous journeys to get anywhere outside of the main urban centers. I knew from experience this trip of roughly 200 kilometers (125 miles) takes six to seven hours, assuming there are no accidents or incidents.

Instead, our host did what most of Guatemala's wealthy elite does —he traveled by private helicopter. After sharing this fact, he enthusiastically went on to tell us how he'd spoken with the women to encourage them in their new handicraft businesses. He explained how he understood just what it was like to be in their position. How he knew that if he wanted to buy an Armani suit like the one he was wearing, he had to work hard for it, just like they would have to work hard. And, he went on, he also understood that the volatility of business markets could be stressful, knowing that some days you made money and other days you didn't.

I've often been told I have a face that does little to hide what I'm feeling. I was conspicuously aware of this fact as I struggled to comprehend what I was hearing. Looking around I wondered, briefly, if this was perhaps some kind of joke. But no. People were nodding and clapping encouragingly.

Keeping my eyes downcast so no one could see the expression on my face, I made my way back out into the relative obscurity of the darkened garden. Trying to calm the tumultuous emotions boiling inside, I took deep gulps. First of the warm night air, and when that failed, from the glass of red wine I still clutched in my hand.

As my pulse slowed and coherent thought began to replace the mad cacophony of monkey brain, it slowly dawned on me. I'd been so excited to have finally met the explicit criteria to be invited into this new social circle that I'd overlooked the implicit criteria. But here it was, all around me. English-speaking, well-educated, Westernized, and everything else that implied. I was there as the Founder of SERES not because of all *I* had achieved. But because Antonio, the one who *should* have been here, wouldn't have been allowed through the door. I put down the glass of wine I'd been holding and walked away.

The next morning I'd scheduled a call with an old colleague in Australia who wanted to help organize a fundraising event for SERES when I made it back home. "You have a great story to tell," he told me. "People will be so inspired to hear about how an Australian woman left everything behind to start an organization in Guatemala and help poor people."

As I thought back to the evening before, my heart dropped to the bottom of my stomach, and a hot red flush came into my cheeks. It's the way my body reacts to deep shame. Was *this* the story I was telling the world? I fumbled my way to the end of the conversation, ended the Skype call, and went outside where I sat down heavily on the concrete steps leading up to my small apartment above the SERES office.

I'd fallen for the old story of change, and fallen hard. It was a story that hangs on the mythology of singular achievement, glorifying the independent hero and their entrepreneurial spirit. We should name it *The Founder Fallacy*. I felt so ashamed, not only of my own hubris, but of the fact I'd been elevating and emulating the work of these "heroic" entrepreneurial changemakers. Invariably some combination of Western, white, wealthy, and well-educated.

I thought about how this message was so at odds with the very values and beliefs on which SERES was founded, that those closest to the problem were the best placed to fix it. Not only that, but in trying to follow in the footsteps of these exalted Leaders, I'd changed so much of what we did and how we did it that I knew the impact we were having wasn't the same.

Driven by my desire to find my place in the old story of change, I'd pursued partnerships with people who didn't have more than three minutes to talk about what we were doing and why it mattered, instead of building deep relationships based on listening and learning. Pushed by outsiders' ideas of what and who had to change, we'd expanded into communities where we knew no one. Places where we hadn't yet built trust. And our team was exhausted from constantly trying to minimize costs and meet unrealistic expectations about budgets and overhead. Instead of being transformative, our work had become transactional.

It's a classic story that's been repeated hundreds–even thousands–of times. A common outcome of our traditional approach to solving change.

I desperately wanted to go back and start again. To rewrite history so it was a different story that I'd heard reflected back to me on the call to Australia. Not about some young Australian woman heroically saving lives, but about the strength and resilience of these brave young people who—against so many seemingly insurmountable odds—were taking a stand to make a difference in their own lives and that of their families and communities.

To do that, I needed to find the courage to take a humble, clear-eyed look at my own complicity.

IT'S IN OUR DNA

Over the course of the last two decades, the world has become increasingly Westernized. A neoliberal ideology has spread around the globe, borne on the wings of an ambitious agenda for economic globalization. It's an ideology that celebrates the ideas of capitalism and the free market, where the number one objective is to maximize profits through continued economic expansion. In doing so it has carried with it many harmful and oppressive worldviews including colonization and colonialism, racial paradigms, patriarchy, growth economics, and extractivism. It's not just monocultural agriculture supported by this kind of philosophy, but monocultural stories about people and their place in the world.

And monocultural narratives, or "single stories" as Nigerian writer Chimamanda Ngozi Adichie calls them, can have disastrous consequences. "Create a single story, show a people as one thing, as only one thing, over and over again, and that is what they become."[2] Like the story of Guatemala's indigenous Maya women. As Adichie argues, the way stories are told, who gets to tell them, and the conditions under which they are told shape the beliefs and ideas we have both about creating change, and the people who need changing. It is a tactic that has been used for decades, all in the name of the Game.

Now when I look back to those early days working with SERES, as I desperately tried to make myself fit into the old story of shaping change, I can identify countless examples of how I was doing just that.

I can see how, for example, the drive for scale is closely tied to a model of infinite economic growth—something that I'd criticized for years. Infinite economic growth is only possible through extractivism: getting the most from materials and resources (including people) without worrying about how to replenish them. It's a pervasive mindset deeply embedded into Western culture, constantly transforming complex relationships and processes into oversimplified transactions and commodifying, well, everything.

What do we do with a commodity? We buy, we sell, and when it is seen to have no more value, we throw it away. That's why we live in a world that treats both people and the planet as disposable. But if I was so opposed to this economic model, what was I doing, I wondered, when I told Antonio that time is money?

And, as I emulated the practices of "successful Leaders," I can see, too, how my increasingly rigid control and planning was connected to a very industrialized command-and-control way of thinking. One that saw the world as linear and predictable and not at all the way that we knew communities—and change process—worked.

I had become more focused on the needs of funders than on the local communities, listening to the advice of people with resources instead of the people with the problem. Driven by those funders' needs for proof of impact, we'd started implementing monitoring and evaluation processes that made our youth feel more like research subjects or naughty children, rather than empowered citizens working on the things that were most important to them.

And, too, I can see that as I tried more and more to be the hero of the story, the people I was working with were relegated to characters that needed to be fixed or saved. As author and historian Rebecca Solnit writes, "The dominant culture mostly goes about reinforcing the stories that are the pillars propping it up and that, too often, are also the bars of someone else's cage."[3]

Acknowledging what I'd done, that I'd been responsible for upholding paradigms I know have been used to oppress and destroy, was difficult. Here I was, yearning for change while sustaining the structural inadequacy of the very systems I was fighting against. All because I didn't stop to examine the foundations and question the assumptions on which our old story of creating change is built.

This is the problem with paradigms: when the values and beliefs enshrined in them don't match with the ethos of the society we're striving to build or the role that we see for ourselves in contributing to that society, they discourage, they dispossess, they disempower. I'd been naive in thinking I could create any change without first stopping to examine the stories I was bringing with me.

I'm aware that the power to shape history—this history—is in my hands. It would be so easy to tell it differently, and who would question it? But too many stories have been papered over in this way, and I, for one, have had enough of heroes. I'm not here to prove myself but improve myself. Which means facing these truths. Because this Game, with its paradigms, is as much part of my reality as it is for youth in Central America and all the other folks who've been pushed out to the margins. An inescapable, unavoidable part of me, part of my story, and part of this story I'm telling you.

WHEN THE INVISIBLE BECOMES VISIBLE

Finding ways to see these invisible forces that shape us and guide our lives is a necessary and powerful step in learning to shape change. Before we can begin choosing the story line about who we want to become, we need to discern the stories we are living and understand the foundations on which they are built.

These foundations carry different names: paradigms, patterns, systems, to name a few. For the sake of clarity and consistency going forward I'll use *patterns* to describe the foundational building blocks. And the scaffolding that upholds them and keeps those patterns alive? Our narratives, stories, tropes, and memes.

I've listed below some examples of the kinds of patterns that I'm talking about. On the left are the old patterns and on the right are new patterns that have been emerging more and more over the last few years. The Weaver's Way framework is designed for the kinds of new patterns that you see in the second list.

OLD STORIES AND PATTERNS || NEW STORIES AND PATTERNS

Old Stories and Patterns	New Stories and Patterns
Competitive individualism	Collaborative community
Transactional relationships	Trust-based relationships
Independent leaders	Interdependent leaders
Hierarchical power structures (maintaining power over)	Distributed/shared power structures, co-leadership models (power with, power to, power within)
Extraction	Regeneration
Globalization	Localization
Gigantism/mass production	Small is beautiful
20th century growth economics	21st century ecological economics and doughnut theory
Expansionary growth	Evolutionary growth
Strategic planning	Emergent strategy
Linear economy	Circular economy
Tribalism with bonding networks	Communities with bridging networks
Trickle down/strong link approaches	Build up/weak link approaches
Charity	Solidarity

As you read through the two lists, you'll probably start to realize how powerful and omnipresent the old patterns are. They lie, like a thick fog blanketing the landscape of our subconscious mind. Deep patterns of thinking and feeling, reinforced and reiterated over our entire lifetimes. You may also start to see that embedded into these patterns are fundamental assumptions about how the world does—or doesn't —work.

It should come as no surprise, therefore, that the first step in shaping meaningful and transformative change is to take time to explore these patterns. Examine the assumptions. And ask yourself— are these the patterns that I want to be following?

As you begin this exploration, pay attention to what happens. In my experience, while these patterns are powerful, it's a power that doesn't bear scrutiny. Like morning fog burning off under the warmth of a winter sun, the power these patterns hold dissipates quickly under a steady, clear-eyed gaze.

AN ODE TO THE BEST GAME IN HISTORY

I recently took a beach holiday with my father and his new girlfriend. It wasn't the best weather for a coastal vacation, with solid rain forecast from sunrise to sunset. In an attempt to allay the cabin fever that started to roll in with the never-ending gray storm clouds, I searched around and pulled out a much-loved game of Jenga. "C'mon," I said to my father, "we'll see what time has done to your skills." As the tower—and the stakes—grew ever higher, I suddenly found myself developing a newfound appreciation for this simple family pastime. "I never realized Jenga held such a good life lesson," I remarked to my father.

"What?" came the puzzled reply.

"Well," I said enthusiastically, "with each block, I'm absolutely certain nothing more can be done. And yet we keep proving ourselves wrong, again and again. It's such a great example of how our beliefs can control our reality, but also how important it is to constantly rethink those beliefs so they don't hold us back."

Dad just shook his head. I don't believe we shared the same appreciation for the finer points of this great game.

As we stacked the blocks for another round, I asked Dad's girlfriend, Gay, if she wanted to join us. Having grown up in Thailand, she didn't have the same childhood appreciation of the game. "Don't worry," I reassured her, "the rules are easy." Perhaps my earlier observations had put me into a more observant frame of mind, but I continued to be fascinated by the insights this relatively simple game had into the Game.

Cultural background wasn't the only thing that set my fellow players apart. There was also the not insignificant age difference and, of course, gender roles—all of which began to play out in front of me. My father, having some experience in building and construction, played Jenga firmly by the building code. Gay, on the other hand, approached it with what—even to me—seemed like reckless abandon, tugging insistently at the first block she laid her hand on.

"You can't do that!" my father would say.

"And yet she just did," I would quip, somewhat triumphantly.

As the tower grew higher, I noticed another shift in my father. For whatever reason, with the three of us now playing, he wasn't prepared to lose. After studying the tower for a couple of minutes he sat back. "There's nothing that can be done," he stated. "I'm out."

Gay and I, less bothered by winning and losing and enjoying the moment, played on. Placing my block, I smiled across at Gay. "Your turn."

But here my father jumped in. Unwilling, it seemed, to risk his own game, he was perfectly prepared to tell Gay what she needed to do.

"She seemed to be doing just fine without your help before," I commented. "If you have an idea, why don't you have another go?"

"No," came the reply. "It's impossible."

The tower inched gradually higher. Once again it was Gay's turn. And once again, my father leaned in to tell her what to do. Frustrated but recognizing it was sensitive territory, I kept quiet and watched as Gay stopped playing her own game and started doing as my dad told her.

The tower came toppling down.

Since that moment of deep shame when I sat on the steps with Antonio and asked him to trust me, I've committed myself to uncovering the patterns that shape who I am and how I see the world. I'd had a painful lesson, and I wanted to avoid making the same mistakes again. With time I became more adept at making the invisible, visible, and seeing how the rules of the Game influenced almost every aspect of my life. There they were in the way I thought about my worth and evaluated my success. Here again in the way I built friendships and related with other people. And there once again, in the way in which I thought about problems and their possible solutions. It's very much a work in progress, but with time and practice it has become easier to see the patterns at work. And, in learning to see these patterns, I'm no longer controlled by them.

Removing the veil of blindness to see things as they really are is a form of resistance to the dominant stories that too often go unquestioned. And that, in turn, is the first step in the remaking of the world.

That game of Jenga held for me so many complex, emotional threads of a difficult childhood and complicated relationship with my father. In a different time, it would've been more than the tower that came crashing down. But in that moment, gathered under the fluorescent lights in the tiny beach shack with the sound of the waves and the rain pressing in, I discovered a newfound sense of freedom. The Game, as it were, goes on, yet it had become just another game, like Jenga. I can choose how I engage, and whether or not I follow the rules. And with that choice comes a sense of lightness and liberation. I am finally free to write my own story.

SUMMARY

- The building blocks for our old stories are based on patterns like patriarchy, colonization, and extractivism. Trying to create change which doesn't address these fundamental worldviews undermines our efforts for true transformation.
- Central to the work of shaping meaningful and transformative change is the requirement to look for and identify where and how these patterns influence us and our proposed solutions and approaches.
- New patterns are possible! There are many new and exciting emerging alternatives built on principles such as abundance, radical generosity, reciprocity, and partnership.

EXERCISES

1. MAKING THE INVISIBLE, VISIBLE.
What patterns are guiding your life?

What are the unwritten rules you play by without ever noticing?
As you become more aware of invisible influences, take the time to
write them down.

2. EXPLORE NEW PARADIGMS.
Use the list below to begin your exploration. Don't worry if you don't
finish it all at once. My own list is in permanent draft form because I'm
always adding to it and updating it. I've learned over the years that
when it comes to patterns, it pays to stay vigilant!

My old stories and patterns:

My new stories and patterns:

3. THINK AGAIN!
Freeing ourselves from the influence of our patterns takes both
curiosity and courage. I've learned to be prepared to constantly
challenge my own assumptions and rethink my beliefs. That isn't
always easy. The following simple "I used to think/Now I think"
exercise can help take the element of shame or judgement out of the
learning/unlearning process.

Each time you have a now-I-see-you moment, simply take a second to
write it down using the format below. Try to be as explicit and
descriptive about what it is that has shifted for you. As you do so you
might find even more that lurks unseen beneath the surface!

I used to think...

Now I think...

4. STAY CURIOUS.

With my own list of old/new patterns, there have been times when I could see the old patterns I wanted to change but didn't know of anything that could yet replace it. For example, after it became clear to us in SERES that operating as a traditional organization wasn't going to work, we started asking ourselves: What does a non-patriarchal, non-hierarchical organizational structure look like that reflects our core values and allows people to feel like they are welcome as their full selves, not just cogs in a machine?[4]

That question helped us learn about a small group of incredible organizations doing just that. They were building truly transformative organizational cultures where it was a joy to turn up each day.

These unknowns offer some of the most exciting edges of innovation for the twenty-first century. So don't be afraid if you come up with something you don't know the answer for. It's an opportunity to add your own ideas, insights, and research. Write it down, and let the question and curiosity carry you forward!

CHAPTER 3
CALLING FORTH THE FUTURE

> When we deny our stories, they define us. When we own our stories, we get to write a brave new ending.
>
> — BRENÉ BROWN

Stories—that's all we are, isn't it? A collection of stories we tell each other. And in the telling of those stories our patterns live, sustained in a dynamic, reinforcing, and interconnected web of ideas, beliefs, values, and relationships.

So what happens when we begin to tell different stories? Stories that use new patterns, ones that reflect the world we are working to create? According to Donella Meadows, one of the world's leading systems thinkers, changing our patterns is the most influential leverage point for creating change.

What happens when we begin to tell different stories is change. Transformative, meaningful, and lasting change.

CHANGE THE STORY, CHANGE THE WORLD

Many years after starting SERES, I was asked in an interview what my superpower was. I thought about it for a moment, then responded, "I know how to believe in people." That may not seem like a big deal, but let me put it into context. When we started SERES, our goal was to support young people from the fringes of society to take action to address the challenges right there in front of them. Just that simple idea was in many ways revolutionary.

Economically and socially marginalized, often denied their most basic human rights and with very limited opportunities to access simple things like education, healthcare, and decent work, who would expect these young people to be capable of—and interested in—creating change? As one young man put it after I'd just finished giving a presentation to a group of employees at a tech company in San Francisco, "It's hard to believe everything they're doing about climate change and gender equality and stuff. I mean, they're poor. I would've thought all that they'd care about is money." It was a statement that came pretty close to capturing how the world saw these young people.

The sad truth was that I'd met very few people in my journey south with as much sense of agency as Antonio. The greatest challenge we faced in our work was that the simple premise—that they *were* capable of creating change—went against just about every story these young people had been led to believe about themselves. Even well-intentioned charitable projects and foreign aid interventions reinforced damaging stereotypes, seeing these youth as a problem that required fixing.

Across Latin America the term *nini* (derived from the Spanish phrase *ni estudian ni trabajan* for those who neither study nor work), was liberally applied to the majority of the region's younger population with little thought, it seems, of the impact this label might have. And, as is typical among populations who have suffered generations of oppression and discrimination, their own self-limiting beliefs simply served to reinforce the story they'd been told. Over and over we heard the same words. "I can't do anything, I'm poor." "I can't make a difference, I'm an indigenous woman." "They won't listen to me, I'm no one."

Tragically, the story of this generation is relegated to the margins before it is even written. Youth coming of age in a time and place where there is no justice. For so many, their reality is one in which life is worth less than a mobile phone, an entire river can be poisoned overnight in the interest of corporate profit, or a voice can be silenced forever just for being female. Worth less and worthless: part of a demographic that has been told over and again they have no value. Is it any wonder these youth had little hope that things would ever be any different, unless by the divine hand of God or the charitable act of some benevolent hero?

Antonio's and my mission when we started SERES was to change this: to help them see change was possible, and that they themselves could play a role in making change happen.

As I learnt from working with Wilbur and his peers, the starting point for changing their story was to redefine the central characters, the so-called Leaders. And so sitting together, discussing what it would take to create change, we asked: What does it mean to lead? What does it mean to have leadership? What does it mean to be a leader? These questions were an invitation to rethink their ideas about leading and leadership, and in doing so to rewrite the stories that defined it. It presented an opportunity to see the world, and their role in it, differently. And with that opportunity, the possibility of creating change.

"A leader," said Wilbur, "is a person who understands the needs of the community and drives actions to work with and for the people." And so with their new definition, Wilbur and other young people just like him suddenly found themselves with a role to play in stopping the unraveling. They did this through organizing neighborhood watches, educational campaigns, after-school activities, learning centers closer to their communities, and communication networks. They became the responsible ones, and through their courage and actions they reclaimed the role of leader and the privilege of shaping change.

Over the ten years that I worked with these communities in Central America, I have witnessed hundreds of young people step through decades of poverty and violence and oppression to claim a new role for themselves, for their generation, and for the generations that followed. From nothing, they found new ways to build power and influence and used this to challenge the injustices all around them. Young women sat in local council seats that had only ever been occupied by male elders. Young men found ways to reach across the ugly tear created by gang violence and state aggression to hold each other and stop the fraying that threatened to unravel their country's fragile social fabric. And youth came together with other generations from across class and culture to form a wall of resistance against the ongoing exploitation and privatization of natural resources.

Their voices and deeds carried from the margins to the center and echoed up to the highest levels of intergovernmental organizations and institutions like UNESCO and the Inter-American Development Bank. And those voices said: change is possible. Because when you change the story, you change the world.

A CURE

I've gone through this same process countless times with people in truly impossible situations. Refugees and migrants, survivors of natural disasters, undocumented students, indigenous girls living in extreme poverty, and young men facing death threats from dangerous criminal gangs. Individuals and populations who have repeatedly been told they have no value. And through this process, into that place of desolation, despair, and demoralizing powerlessness, they wrote a new story and called forth a new future.

None of these people would have been considered Leaders (big L), but they all went on to create and lead change in their communities and places of origin that contributed toward building a fairer, more hopeful future for themselves and others like them.

Working alongside them dramatically influenced my ideas about leading and leadership. Core to these ideas is the simple premise that leadership is a disposition rather than a position, which is reflected each moment of the day in the way we work and walk in this world. It's a subtle but important shift in perspective when it comes to change, making the privilege of shaping change as inclusive and accessible as the old way was exclusive and elite.

I use the word privilege with great intentionality. Because shaping change should not—is not—the domain of our bosses, managers, or elected officials. It *is* a privilege, and one that we must claim.

I have heard this idea described as revolutionary, but I prefer to think of it as evolutionary: a timely and necessary response to the situation we are in as a civilization, that has left so many of us denying ourselves the ability to take action on the things that are most important to us. And it is the perfect antidote to the twenty-first century malaise of hopelessness and helplessness.

The stories we tell about ourselves and each other have a powerful effect on our lives and our work. And the shaping of our identity is intimately tied to those story lines. When we find a way to create new stories, stories that empower us to take full responsibility for the world around us, we come alive. We re-engage with the world in a way that connects us to our true, authentic selves. And with that connection comes the power to shape change and the world we live in.

I know this is possible because I've seen this process time and again, working in the trenches with some of the world's most disempowered individuals and communities. People who strove to overcome the narratives that history had handed them and write a new story for themselves and their future. I know it's possible because I did it with my own story.

ANTONIO FOUND ME AFTER THAT REVEALING SKYPE CALL STILL SITTING ON THE steps. Another rush of shame washed over me when I saw him. I rubbed at my face, trying to remove the salt that had crystallized in the corners of my eyes, making me feel as worn and dried out on the outside as I felt on the inside.

Alarmed, he asked me what was wrong.

"When did this become so hard?" I asked him. "What happened to the meaning? The joy?"

He sighed and sat down on the step below me. "I don't know. Isn't that the way it works?" There was a long pause while we both stared off into the distance.

"And what have I been doing telling people I'm the Founder of SERES?" I asked him. "It should be you."

He turned now to look at me, slightly bewildered. "Of course not. You've worked so hard. You're the one who built the organization, developed the programs, and raised the money."

I thought with sadness just how much that entrepreneurial hero story had influenced all of us, even down to determining what efforts were deemed more worthy of recognition than others. "And you," I countered, "are the heart and soul of what we do. You are the relationships, the connections, the communities, the context. What is this without you?" I thought about the event the evening before. "It's nothing but fancy words."

We started talking then about how we'd gotten here. What decisions we'd made, and the reasons for making those decisions. About doors which had opened to us and how, in walking through those doors, we'd accepted certain story lines about ourselves and the work. And we discussed what it signaled to the outside world when we used titles such as founder and executive director, and what it signaled to us as well.

"It just seems like such a game," said Antonio. There it was again, *the Game.* The Game we are all playing, handed our roles without even realizing. What would happen if we chose not to play?

We sat together for a few moments in silence. "What if we start again, rewrite history?" I asked him. A pause. "Would you accept me as your cofounder?" There was a much longer pause this time. I was asking for *me* to become *we.* I was asking for his consent. I was asking for his trust. But was I trustworthy?

"Please?"

Antonio's eyes met mine, and he took a deep breath. "Okay." His smile matched my own.

BLUEPRINT FOR CHANGE

Since we are in the process of rewriting stories and changing history, there is another important story that needs to be retold. That of Guatemala's women weavers. Their story is one of strength, resilience and resistance. Of beauty and endurance. Of culture and connection. But it is, in fact, much more than a story.

Weaving is one of the oldest surviving human practices and a foundational cornerstone of many cultures. For thousands of years, in almost every society, weavers have made an invaluable contribution to culture and identity, creating objects of art, beauty, and everyday use. Not just practical, a weaver's work helps to tell stories, confer status, and give context and, in many cases, the fruits of their labors have outlived the society from which they came. Weaving imparts meaning and understanding across time and space, sustaining the thread of our common human connection.

The roots of weavers trace back to early mythologies of many different cultures including the Greeks, Egyptians, Native Americans, and many others. With the exception of the Christian church and its saints, most of these mythologies associated different goddesses with elements of weaving, which in turn were connected to the creation and nurturing of life and creativity, fertility, abundance, and other elements. It is even believed that in Ancient Egyptian hieroglyphics, the root of the word for weaving is the same as that for being *(nnt)*.

Is it any wonder, then, that equally as important as the literal weavers to our communities and society at large are the metaphorical Weavers? The metaphorical idea of Weaving is scattered throughout history, often in connection with broader social movements. But while Weavers' contribution to society, both literal and metaphorical, cannot be disputed, the importance of this role itself has been largely overlooked and undervalued.

Remember Guatemala's indigenous women weavers? Despite being the quintessential, iconic representation of the country, as well as their indisputable importance as the cultural custodians of a practice that is over two thousand years old, they are amongst the most marginalized and oppressed demographics in the region.

A similar story can be seen with the metaphorical Weaver. As we have explored in previous chapters, our societal patterns and cultural narratives have favored stories that promoted the entrepreneurial individualistic hero. While these Leaders have been held responsible for the revolutions and counter revolutions that have moved us forward (and sometimes backward) through abrupt technological, social and political changes, the quietly determined work of Weavers transformed revolution into evolution, weaving these changes into our social fabric so they could be sustained and nurtured, and allowing them to become part of the rich tapestry of our combined history.

For too long, the vital work that Weavers have done has been overlooked and forgotten. It's time for the Weavers and their stories to be given a new place in our history books. And not just any old place. Front and center. Because Weaving is our blueprint for change.

This blueprint isn't new. In fact, it's as old as our civilization itself.

At the beginning of the first century, Jewish religious leader, sage, and scholar Rabbi Hillel gave a teaching wherein he posed three questions to his followers. Hillel asked:

If I am not for myself, who am I?

When I am only for myself, what am I?

And if not now, when?

It may have been a long time ago, but these questions are just as relevant now as they were then.

Hillel's call to action asks us to examine three ideas together: What am I called to do, what are others with whom I am in relationship called to do, and what action does the world in which we live demand of us now? It is the recognition for the interdependence of self, other, and action, and it is fundamental to our blueprint for change.

PERHAPS ONE OF THE BIGGEST FALLACIES OF THE OLD CHANGE NARRATIVE WITH its independent hero is the idea any one of us can do it alone. Solving the complex, interconnected challenges we face today requires more than the work of a handful of Leaders. It requires a movement of leaders from across race, religion, class, gender, and geography. A leader-*full* generation.

This new blueprint for change—the framework that we'll explore together in Part II—represents a shift in values. Away from hyper-individualism and the pursuit of personal success to a success that puts the wellbeing of all living things in the center. It is longitudinal, collective, and grounded in care: focused on the wellbeing of all people and the planet over time. And it is the foundation from which we can begin to write new stories—with new stars—about how to shape change. Starting now.

OUR STORY: THE WEAVING EVOLUTION

Working with Wilbur and others like him has given me an acute awareness that history is happening around me every day. Right now, even, on these pages. At this very moment.

Yes, history is the combined sum of our actions (and inactions), echoing down the hallways to our children's children and grandchildren, and all those who will follow after. But it is also a selective record of what we choose to tell about those deeds. The goal of Wilbur and his peers was to rewrite their story so they were no longer victims, helpless and hopeless. But in doing so, in living and telling a different story, one in which they had the power, position, permission, and perspective to shape change, they rewrote history.

We can do the same.

Take note next time you sit down for a cup of coffee or a shared meal with friends or family. Does the conversation lead to what is broken, or to what is new and emerging?

When we spend all our time talking about what's not working, we continue to nurture and nourish the old, ossified ways of doing and being. It is time to shift the conversation. To let go of the stories of the past and be part of a new narrative for the future. Because it is only through the regeneration and recreation of our stories and beliefs about the world and each other that we will begin to create a free, fair, and flourishing home for life in all its manifestations.

"Stories have been used to dispossess and to malign, but stories can also be used to empower and to humanize. Stories can break the dignity of a people, but stories can also repair that broken dignity," says Chimamanda Ngozi Adichie[1]. We need to breathe life into those stories, make a conscious effort to shift our patterns of thinking and our ways of being away from the old and toward the new. To let people like Wilbur inspire and encourage us to step into the new story. To live it and breathe it and speak it.

Imagine for a moment a world where everyone has the chance to live a safe and dignified life. Where the planet is thriving and whole again. Where trust is the currency and reciprocity the language that connects us. A world where our relationships are inclusive, generous, and engaging, and we all take responsibility to ensure there is space to listen, and to be heard. A world where there is respect for all people and all of life.

Change is a force that is constantly shaping our lives, but how often do we think about shaping that very same change? Building a better world is not someone else's job: it's all our jobs.

It's time to give ourselves a new story, one that embraces a new way of leading and leadership and allows us to claim the privilege of shaping change. "Who am I to create change?" you may ask. Who are you *not* to?

Everything we know about this world so far is a story told or written by someone. So who will you let dictate your story?

Wilbur made the difficult decision not to leave and migrate north because he was determined to write another story. "If we don't change it," he said, "no one else will." It may be that he was talking to us.

So, what have we covered in Part I? We've discussed the need for a new narrative of change for the twenty-first century, a narrative built on an understanding of the world as interdependent and interconnected. We also talked about the fact that our new narrative is not singular but a collection of stories that honors our diversity. This new narrative embraces plurality and contradiction, seeking emergence rather than settling for certainty. It is a narrative focused on building community bridges rather than tribal bonds, helping us to connect with people who may be different but who nevertheless hold that same wish for a thriving future, a more beautiful world.

This new collection of stories can help to heal, to hold together the fabric of society against the divisive forces that would tear us asunder, repairing the tired and frayed edges that are becoming too thin and fragile to hold in safekeeping all of those who dwell at the margins. These stories help us to see that whoever we are, and wherever we stand, we have the power, permission, position, and perspective to shape change.

But this collection of stories, this new narrative, isn't really new. It is as old as the Greek and Egyptian goddesses of mythology. It is the story of The Weavers, old and new, near and far, who are doing the work to build more participatory democracies, inclusive societies, and equitable futures for all. Will it be your story?

SUMMARY

- When we begin to create new stories, we engage with the world in a way that connects us to our true, authentic selves. With that comes the possibility to shape the world we live in.
- Finding ways to positively contribute toward your community and the world is the perfect antidote to the twenty-first century malaise that has left so many of us denying ourselves the ability to take action on the things that are most important to us.
- Shaping change doesn't require you to drop everything, quit your job, and become a martyr for a cause. Look around you and notice the abundance of opportunities for making the world a better place.

EXERCISES

1. YOUR STORY OF SELF.

Often we're not aware of the stories we tell ourselves. One way to become more aware is to use the exercises in the previous chapter. Another way is to ask someone close to you to reflect back what they hear in your stories.

2. FIND SOMEONE YOU TRUST.

Explain to them that you are trying to identify dominant themes that make up your story of self. Try to put aside any inclination to shaming or blaming by getting curious. Try to see the patterns by looking for similarities and trends. What are you noticing?

3. CHALLENGE YOUR STORIES.

Can you see ways in which these stories might influence how you see yourself and your ability to shape change? What would it take to let go of those stories? What might be possible if you did?

PART TWO
WE, THE WEAVERS

CHAPTER 4
A WEAVING METAPHOR

> Go to the people. Live with them. Learn from them. Love them. Start with what they know. Build with what they have.
>
> — LAO TZU

The *Weaver's Way* is a blueprint for shaping change, one that harnesses our deep inner instinct for connection and caring. It is presented in this book as a framework, which develops the idea of weaving for change beyond a simple metaphor into something more structured that can help you learn how to shape change that is meaningful, transformative, and aligned with the values and beliefs upon which a more just and equitable future can be created. But before we begin to explore this in more detail, a note on frameworks themselves.

It is important to understand that a framework is not a prescriptive how-to. There are no answers built in. *The Weaver's Way* is not another leadership strategy to be consumed, or a quiz that will give you your strengths and weaknesses. Nor will it provide any easy five-step formula to follow.

What it will do is to help you to break through long-established patterns of thought and behavior. You can think of *The Weaver's Way* framework like the set of equipment in a children's playground. What do children do on that equipment? They use it to test their limits, to hang upside down and see the world from a different perspective. To push boundaries and challenge power structures (all those tantrums when it's time to leave). To interact with others, to use their imaginations to make up new stories, and, ultimately, to play and have fun.

You can—and should—do the same with this framework.

The purpose of the framework is to help you to see things differently when it comes to shaping change, to provide a structure that can help you understand all the different dimensions and complexities of whatever issue you choose to engage with. And to discover a deeper sense of meaning and worth while you do it.

For this framework to have any significant impact, it is important that you test it through your own lived experience. You can read about slipping down a slide or hanging from the monkey bars, but you won't really know what it is like until you actually do it. The same applies here. Use this framework as an invitation, a provocation, an opportunity. There is no right or wrong. Be open and curious: pilot the concepts, explore where they lead, and take the time afterward to reflect on what happened. Remember, your story is part of the collective, and your differences and unique experiences are vital in co-creating our new narrative.

As we move into the framework, we'll explore two distinct but interconnected aspects of the metaphor: The *Weaver* as a role or identity and the characteristics that define the role, and *Weaving* as an act or a way of working and the guidelines for how to approach that work. Being and doing or, as I often say, the way that you walk and work in the world. Inseparably intertwined.

This framework recognizes that the dynamic interrelationship between inner life and the outer world is a fundamental aspect in shaping transformational change.

As you strengthen your ability to look at the world through the eyes of The Weaver, you'll find yourself approaching situations more often using the tools of Weaving. Conversely, as you practice the work of Weaving, you'll find you deepen your ability to see things through The Weaver lens. This is the beauty of the two concepts: mutually inclusive, self-reinforcing, regenerative.

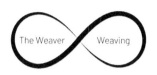

The Weaver's Way Framework

Some of the ideas presented in *The Weaver's Way* framework may seem awkward or uncomfortable at first. That discomfort simply means you're trying something new. Becoming familiar with them will take time and practice.

It will also mean questioning your own mental maps, challenging assumptions, and asking yourself "What do I know to be true?" That in and of itself is a good skill to build. Becoming skilled at shaping meaningful and transformative change is as much about unlearning and relearning as it is about learning. Core abilities that, according to the futurist Alvin Toffler, are as fundamental to our twenty-first century context as reading and writing[1].

WEAVER AS A META-IDENTITY

The shaping of identity is closely tied to the story lines that a particular society makes available and desirable to its members. One of the most significant consequences, therefore, of single stories and monocultural narratives are that they limit what identities are deemed acceptable, worthy and appropriate. We develop a handful of generic identities, matched to the sparse smattering of story lines.

One of the most extreme examples I ever saw of this was when I first started working in Guatemala at a time when we were visiting a lot of primary schools. As I chatted with the kids, I would invariably ask them the age-old-question: what do you want to be when you grow up? In ninety-nine percent of cases I received only one of two answers. Teacher was the most common, and every now and then, an extremely ambitious young man would say architect.

But even in Western society the same is true. The characters within our stories do much to influence how we move through the world, our relationship to others, and the work we do. Consequently, we are both limited in the identities available to us and limited in what is considered appropriate behavior when we assume those identities.

I am thinking of two somewhat well-known examples: Julia Gillard (Australia's first female prime minister) and Jacinta Ardern (New Zealand's currently serving prime minister). During Julia Gillard's time as Leader, both media and opposition party leaders were far more interested in discussing her wardrobe, marital status, and general presentation than they were discussing her policies. Society, it seemed, just couldn't get past the identity that an Australian woman of Julia Gillard's age was supposed to have.

While Jacinda Ardern has—thankfully—received far less criticism and harassment, we nevertheless know far more about her mothering practices than we ever have about the equivalent male heads of state's relationship to their families.

For many of us, the limitation of identities can feel akin to being forced to wear a mask. We carry one for our professional lives, one for our personal lives, and all too often, another when we look in the mirror. But wearing masks limits our ability to create authentic connection and engage fully with the world around us.

So what happens when we take them off?

A few years back I was invited as a guest speaker to a class of final-year business students on social finance. For part of the class I asked the students to think about and discuss their own money story. As they began talking among themselves, a wonderful transformation took place. From a somewhat sterile start typical of the online classroom, little by little the professional student masks fell away as a beautiful storytelling process unfolded.

We heard the story of a student born of immigrant parents, of the daughter of a single mum, as well as accounts of growing up wealthy and being terrified of poverty. As the students shared these intimate stories, they began not only to uncover their own layers of identity but to see each other with more depth and understanding. A rich dialogue ensued about how these different identities informed their relationship(s) with money and how those relationships would undoubtedly impact their decisions and actions in their future careers and beyond. One student later reached out to me to share that the insight gained from our session was one of the most important lessons she would take from her studies.

Just as with those students, when we have the opportunity to remove our masks it not only allows us to access the wisdom and lived experience of our different identities, but it also permits a greater awareness of the deeper narratives that shape those identities. And, as we discussed in Part I, being aware of those narratives will help us to choose the stories we wish to live and to tell. It also brings us close to connecting with our ability to shape meaningful and transformative change.

I like to think of the Weaver as a kind of meta-identity—all-encompassing, under which we can feel free to be our authentic selves. As Weavers, we see each other for who we truly are, acknowledging the rich plurality of our inner diversity. And we allow ourselves and each other to show up as our whole selves, bringing with us the stories, histories, cultures, beliefs that make each and every one of us unique. To see how that works in practice, I'd like to introduce you to Joyce Yee, our first Weaver from the Weaver's Guild. Joyce Yee is an associate professor from the Northumbria University School of Design. You'll read more about her research and work later in the book, but for now I want to share Joyce's own journey with discovering her identities and embracing the Weaver.

WEAVER: JOYCE YEE

Joyce's early career follows a fairly typical trajectory. Originally from Malaysia, Joyce did her professional design training in the UK in the mid 1990s before returning home to practice as a designer for a top Malaysian design agency. "Back then," says Joyce "the applications of design were fairly limited: It was all about making stuff in a corporate, commercial context." But for Joyce, it felt empty. "I had a sense that design could do more, but I didn't know what that was."

That general sense of discontent led Joyce back to the world of academia and into research where she became more curious about the role of design. "What called to me was the potential of design beyond making stuff." As she researched and explored, Joyce began to see how limited the mainstream design discourse was. "The design heroes that you learn about, they are the same tropes that you find everywhere. I could name them all, and they're mainly white men. Design's story was one of the individual hero, and at the time there wasn't a lot of critical self-reflection questioning that story. The idea of working with the community with collaborative ideas was unheard of."

It was around that same time that design began to expand into other areas like service and policy design. Watching this shift got Joyce wondering. "I was thinking that perhaps design could be used for a social good, if we stopped thinking about products and services and focused more on design as an enabler to support others to enact change." But it was hard. "Like...the intention was there, but the modeling didn't fit."

Joyce was beginning to experience that uncomfortable, existential pull when we are confronted by two conflicting narratives. "My education and learning taught me that design was primarily aimed at serving commercial needs, so when I kept looking at design as something that could have a social good, it was hard to reconcile the tools, methods, and practices that I was used to into a completely different context. How do you shift from designing desirable things to designing the (socio-technical-material) infrastructures to enable change? It wasn't just the context that was different; it required a fundamental change to how we viewed the world. I realized that as designers, we weren't trained to think that way. We didn't have the sensitivity for it."

As I listened to Joyce talk about this sense of not fitting, I'm reminded of the masks that so many of us feel we are forced to wear in professional and even social settings. For Joyce, her professional identity as a designer, and the narrative that went alongside it, was based largely on the experiences of white men. But what could design look like expressed through her own, authentic identities?

Joyce realized she needed to look inside: to examine the stories and narratives that she'd adopted through her education and training that influenced her own way of thinking about design, and to critically examine the design paradigm that shaped the way she approached her work.

This was the beginning of a slow pivot that brought her back to her roots and connected her with her heritage. She met Dr. Yoko Akama, a Western-educated Japanese designer based in Australia, and together they started DESIAP.

DESIAP became the vehicle for Joyce's own journey, an opportunity to explore and express her profession through her different identities. As she did, she finally found what she'd been looking for: a starting point to discover how to use design for social good.

Together with Dr. Akama, she sought to highlight how design was being imported into local practices and sold as a product, without consideration of whether it was culturally appropriate. Their aim with DESIAP was to challenge these dominant practices and to advocate for other forms of locally relevant practices that may not be considered design in the formal sense. With this came a newfound sense of what was possible. "I began to recognize designing in other forms, beyond what I was taught as 'design.' This opened up multiple (and still emerging) ways for me to consider how design can support place-based strategies for creating change."

Through the process, Joyce has also learned to develop the sensitivity she felt was missing in her formal education. I asked her to tell me more about what she has discovered.

"In order to work in this way, you need to be very honest about your positionality and be open to vulnerability, especially when needing to challenge your assumptions and intentions, because you aren't separate from the act. You're a part of it. You need to stop and question why are you there? What are your politics when working in that space? What are you trying to achieve? Traditional design education teaches us how to do something, which then translates into what, but we miss the why and for whom. That reflexivity and criticality, knowing why you are doing it…it's just so important."

The way that Joyce approaches shaping change has now shifted dramatically from how she was taught. "It's about recognizing what's there. Asking ourselves, what can we learn from this? What can I offer to support and build on what is already here? The starting point is different. Instead of approaching a situation with a problem-solving mindset, it starts by listening, attuning to, and being sensitive to who's in the room (and also who's not in the room)."

In order to really start designing, she explains, she needed to let go of her identity as a designer.

Through that process, Joyce began to question and reconnect her other identities. "I'm Malaysian-Chinese, and I've lived now in the UK for longer than I have in Malaysia. This creates different, sometimes contradictory, identities. I'm an immigrant. But I'm also an ethnic Chinese…" Her words drift off as they are caught up in some internal train of thought. "There are so many complex interactions between these identities."

Joyce's journey also prompted her to look more into decolonial and feminist theories. "Unless you realize the systems and structures hidden there, you can't question them. You don't stop to question where your tools and practices come from and whether they help or whether they continue to support the existing structures of oppression or injustice."

Listening to Joyce speak, I'm reminded by a recent interview with organizational psychologist and author Adam Grant about his new book, *Think Again.* "It takes curiosity to learn. It takes courage to unlearn."[2] I appreciate the courage in Joyce's own story.

After finally reaching the peak of her professional career (although Joyce is quick to clarify that there is no peak if we accept that learning is an ongoing process), she is now learning new languages with which to critique it. She is also learning the language with which she can tell a new story.

"For such a long time, it wasn't that I was burying my identities, but they just didn't seem relevant." And yet in opening up to the complex layers of her identity, she has come closer to her purpose, and discovered a way that design can be used as a force to shape transformative change and create social good. "This journey enabled me to bring together multiple strands of my personal and professional practice to find ways to use design for social good."

Joyce had become a Weaver.

THE SUBSEQUENT WORK THAT JOYCE HAS DONE THROUGH DESIAP IS MAKING an invaluable contribution to providing clear, evidence-based research that demonstrates just what is possible when we embrace a new narrative around shaping change. But what I find insightful about Joyce's story is that she found her calling only after she stepped out of the monocultural expression of her professional life and began to explore her work through her different identities.

We all have multiple layers that make up our identities and realities. Becoming a Weaver is not about adopting another rigid identity that overshadows all others. It's about creating a space wherein your multiplicity of identities—all of them—are welcome. Despite the fact that many work cultures and social norms do not acknowledge or embrace this wonderful richness, I've found that it's often the experiences associated with the less-recognized identities that brings the strength and nuanced understanding that makes our work truly transformative.

So welcome. All of you.

SUMMARY

- *The Weaver's Way* framework for shaping change and solving complex problems draws on ancient wisdom and knowledge and is designed to help us find solutions for the complex twenty-first century problems we face.
- The framework has two distinct but interconnected aspects: The Weaver as a role and *Weaving* as an act or a way of working. These two concepts are mutually inclusive, self-reinforcing, and regenerative.
- Being a Weaver is a meta-identity. We all have many, multiple-layered identities. Becoming comfortable with these identities brings us closer to our ability to shape meaningful and transformative change.

EXERCISES

1. EMBRACE YOUR IDENTITIES.
Take a pen and write down all of your different identities. My list may look something like: woman, sister, daughter, Australian, engineer, facilitator, writer, explorer. On any given day, it may include from ten to twenty different identities depending how I am feeling/what identities are speaking to me.

How many identities are on your list? How do these identities impact your work and the way you shape change? In what circumstances is any particular identity more or less dominant?

2. CONSIDER CONTEXT.
Being a wife in Australia is very different from being a wife in

Guatemala because the cultural narratives around a wife's role are very different. At a more meta level, however, there are similarities. Both Australia and Guatemala are deeply influenced by a patriarchal pattern. As such, being a wife in Australia or Guatemala is very different from being a wife among Indonesia's indigenous Minangkabau for example, which is a self-identified matriarchy.

How does context shape the things you do and say within a particular identity?

Do you find this context oppressive or liberating? How might changing context (e.g., a different country or culture) change your experience of this identity?

3. Masks off!
Joyce's story shows us how being connected to ourselves, grounded in our identities is powerful. When we are clear about who we are, we open up the possibility of relating to everyone else. We approach people more able to listen, more able to create genuine connections rather than searching for validation.

This can only happen when we are prepared to remove our masks and invite others to do the same. It can happen in the smallest of ways. Next time you meet someone, try asking them what they are passionate about or what they are good at rather than what they do.

These kinds of questions invite people to remove their masks and show up more authentically. What kinds of rituals, invitations, or questions could you use to do this at work, at home, or socially?

CHAPTER 5
THE WEAVER'S WAY

 May I learn all the ways in which I do not really see you.
All the ways I rush through you, past you, over you. May
I learn to pause in your presence.

— CHANI NICHOLAS

In beginning to explore weaving as a framework for shaping change, I find it useful to think about the mechanics of weaving in a literal sense. There are an incredible number of different loom types, which is unsurprising given its rich and diverse history. Yet the one I'm most familiar with is the backstrap loom, which thousands of Guatemalan Maya women have used for centuries. Women like Loida.

Loida Juana Cholotío is T'zutujil Maya. Born in 1948, she is one of two children and herself a mother of six. Abandoned by her father at the age of three after her mother died in childbirth, she grew up in her maternal grandparents' house. Speaking only T'zutujil at home, Loida never had the opportunity to go to school or learn to read and write. As such, her Spanish is as limited as her world, which doesn't stretch far beyond the shores of Lake Atitlán. It's a fitting setting for our book: one of the world's most beautiful lakes nestled, in quintessential Guatemalan juxtaposition, within one of the poorest areas in the country.

Abigail is Loida's daughter. Two generations of Maya women, both weavers. But while Loida's is the literal work of weaving for practical use and income generation, Abigail's is the work of Weaving, shaping change. The resilience and resistance passed down for years from generation to generation of women has been transformed in Abigail. She was the first young indigenous woman I worked with when I started SERES. As a young leader (known as a Youth Ambassador) within the SERES movement, Abigail founded Casa Maya, a social business that provides economic empowerment to indigenous women. And when I stepped down from the leadership of SERES, she stepped up as co-executive director.

It is through Abigail that I've come to know Loida, and while language has kept Loida and me from communicating directly, our connection is the tender bond of two people who love and cherish the same human being: her daughter. I owe much of the insight, learning, and experience that I share in this book to these threads of connection between Loida, Abigail, and myself. Threads that stretch out across language, culture, and generations to embrace a common understanding that is rooted in our collective humanity.

I first met Abigail in 2010. Since that time, we've spent many hours in conversation. An emerging and evolving relationship from newly made acquaintances to coworkers to friends to flatmates until finally settling into the enduring comfort and connection of two people whose souls have seen each other. It was within the trust and safety of that relationship that we explored many of the ideas that have formed and informed the foundation of *The Weaver's Way*.

We traveled together through the often emotionally fraught fields of difference, covering topics such as race, religion, power, privilege, and many others, gifted with the kinds of tender and vulnerable conversations that can only happen where there is true love, respect, trust, and safety. It was this shared journey that helped me to discover and experience firsthand many of the concepts presented in *The Weaver's Way* framework.

In the sense-making phase that I underwent as research for this book, I spent more time in conversation with Loida (through Abigail) to learn more about the actual practice of weaving. Within those conversations, I found many pearls of wisdom that have helped me to better understand my own work as a Weaver of change and the greater framework. I have arranged those pearls of wisdom into five principles which make up the first part of *The Weaver's Way* framework.

But first, I'd like you to meet Loida.

LOIDA JUANA CHOLOTÍO

Loida comes out of the kitchen to weave, and a couple of rust-red chickens scatter out of her way with an indignant squawk. At just under 1.4 m in height (around 4'7"), she is fairly typical of a demographic for whom chronic malnutrition is a childhood constant, leading to the highest prevalence of stunting among under-five children in Latin America. Her long black hair flecked with gray is plaited down her back and tied with a bright ribbon, which matches the handmade indigenous dress that is her daily outfit. She has her loom in her hand, a bundle of "sticks and strings" as I once heard from a passing tourist.

It is true though. When carried this way it could easily be mistaken for a confused jumble of yarn and wooden rods. But once you see it in situ, you quickly recognize the simple yet complicated tool that it is—a trademark of both literal and metaphorical weaving, as any systems thinker would recognize.

The backstrap loom is so named because of the strap that wraps around the weaver's back, fixing the loom in front of them to do their work. As Loida prepares to weave, she ties one end of the loom to a wooden post. It is the corner of the covered walkway that encircles the patio of their small housing complex. She spreads her small mat onto the dirt floor. Then, with the exaggerated precision of one whose body is a reservoir of accumulated memories—each with its own physical reminder—she slowly sits down, careful not to spill a drop.

She wraps the strap of the loom around her back. Still not faded despite years of wearing, the purple-and-white-striped strap contrasts beautifully with the aquamarine blue of her *güipil* (Mayan blouse) and the vivid tree-green-yellow blend of her skirt.

The chickens wander around the courtyard, picking caterpillars and bugs off the trees and plants growing there, disturbed and disturbing now and then with the occasional squawk as one of Loida's five dogs or seven grandchildren wander by. This house was once among the poorest in the village, but through the economic support of her children, Loida's home now has electricity, running water, a flushing toilet, and a refrigerator—things she didn't have growing up in the fifties.

Another one of those comforts is the low, three-legged stool on which she now sits, bare feet stretched out in front of her. In her hand is a small rod, wound with the yarn she will be using, as well as a big stick which she uses to beat the weft (the actual weaving) with each pass of the shuttle. The loom rises sharply at an angle in front of her, a collection of brightly colored possibilities.

With everything in place, Loida begins to weave. As she does so, she shows us the weaver's way, demonstrating the five guiding principles that underpin *The Weaver's Way*.

PRINCIPLE I: DANCE WITH TENSION

The rhythm of weaving overtakes her body. Her torso moves back and forth to increase and relax the tension on the warps, the shuttle flicks from side to side, and her arms respond with the downward thump-thump as the warp is beaten into place. Side to side, in and out, thump thump. Side to side, in and out, thump thump. Loida weaves with the quiet confidence of someone who has mastered her craft. Watching her, with the repetitive rhythm and hands dancing in and out of the colored threads, it is easy to become wrapped up in the time-standing-still peaceful calm that comes with the intense concentration of an artist at work.

As I observe Loida, I'm reminded that the essence of a weaver's work is the creative and constructive use of tension. Knowing how to hold it in her body, how to transmit it in her work, how to play with it between the individual strands. Line by line, Loida draws in the different threads, inviting them into a coherent unity.

It is at once practical and artistic. Practical, in that the test of success lies in Loida's ability to tie those threads together in a way that's strong and resilient, withstanding the test of time. Artistic because the intricacy and richness of the finished weaving lies in the detail and her ability to bring out the unusual colors or patterns.

The same applies to the metaphorical Weaver, whose work is to use tension constructively and creatively to bring forth new solutions. *The Weaver's Way* framework is one that values collaboration over competition. But creating a truly collaborative environment isn't free from conflict. Disagreement is a natural part of the human experience. How we handle those disagreements and differences is what determines whether an environment is adversarial, conflicted, and hostile; conflict-avoiding and passive aggressive; or collaborative and supportive.

Imagine for a moment a simple scenario. There's a car driving down the street. One side, the left, is painted white. The other side is painted black. Straight down the middle. Two observers stand on opposite sides of the street. Later, they're asked to describe the car. One declares it was white. The other vows it was black. It is a scenario that is repeated in a million ways, every day. We forget the vital role of perspective. The Weaver asks: Is there a place wherein both of these statements could be true and if so, how do we get there?

Being able to ask this question is a reflection of the Weaver's ability to hold and play with tension. This is sometimes referred to as integrative thinking. Roger Martin, a former dean of the Rotman School of Management at the University of Toronto and author of

When More Is Not Better: Overcoming America's Obsession with Economic Efficiency, defines integrative thinking as "the ability to face constructively the tension of opposing ideas and, instead of choosing one at the expense of the other, generate a creative resolution of the tension in the form of a new idea that contains elements of the opposing ideas but is superior to each."[1] Martin believes being able to hold two conflicting ideas in constructive tension and then use that tension to generate new solutions is one of the key characteristics of a successful twenty-first-century leader. It is certainly a core skill of Weavers.

Developing these skills is part of the inner journey of becoming a Weaver, which I discuss further in the next chapter. But for Loida, being able to dance with tension comes down to learning how to tender humility, the second guiding principle of the framework.

PRINCIPLE 2: TENDER HUMILITY

Tender (verb): to present for acceptance, to make a proposal of.

An admission of guilt from a type A perfectionist. I have the habit of scribbling notes and ideas from conversations and meetings onto random scraps of paper, economizing on space through imaginative changes of both color and direction. The result normally looks a little like one of my three-year-old niece's drawings. If I'm honest, it can make for a frustrating process when finding any specific notes down the track, as I comb through pile after pile of mismatched pieces of paper covered with red, blue, and black scrawls all going in different directions.

But every now and then, this unsystematic filing system is vindicated. Like on this occasion, when I was looking back to find some notes from a meeting with a client and two words jumped off the page at me:

TENDER HUMILITY.

At the time, I had been speaking with Abigail about a concept that we were struggling to translate from T'zutujil to Spanish. I've found this to be a common challenge when translating between languages that come from different paradigmatic worldviews when it's not just the words, but the frame of reference that requires translating. Many indigenous words, for example, don't have exact analogue equivalents in colonizer languages such as English, French, or Spanish. Conversely, they also have no words for the impact these cultures have had on the world, like climate change or global warming.

After about thirty minutes and many different examples, we'd come to the conclusion that the closest translation to *tino'y riil* was tenderness + humility. Or *tender humility,* as I'd written down. But now, as I glanced at the words once again my brain had registered the word *tender* not as an adjective, but as a verb. With this idea in mind, I went back to my notes from the conversation with Loida. At the time, we had been talking about the act of kneeling.

Traditionally, and still the case for many, women did their weaving kneeling down on the hard-packed dirt floor. I had always been moved by the humility of this act, to kneel for hours in service to your work. I shared my observation with Loida and asked her to tell me more about the act of kneeling and the idea of humility. It is not humility, she said, it is *tino'y riil*, the essence of a weaver. Similar, but different.

The women who weave are invaluable to their families and to our community. They are the guardians of unique wisdom and skill. And they are the ones whose work inspires younger generations to dream. To do this they must have tino'y riil.

Tino'y riil is synonymous with the spirit of service from the heart. When someone has tino'y riil, they aren't blinded by how important they think they are, what family they are from, or what position they hold. It doesn't matter how intelligent they think they are. You must practice tino'y riil constantly, especially whenever you interact with someone else.

Abigail tries to explain it to me in her own words:

It means knowing how to make yourself small so that you can truly attend to the person in front of you. For example, if I walk past an elder in the street I don't just stop to greet them. I slow down and allow my own steps to accompany their rhythm for as long as our paths are together. I am smiling and attentive, my whole body is listening. I am not distracted by anything. And when I receive people in my home, I receive them with the same level of hospitality, regardless of who they are or where they come from or how important they are supposed to be.

When we are able to tender humility in service to our work and the community it becomes easier to accept and acknowledge that we don't have all of the answers. This can be a frightening proposition in a world that demands certainty. But one secret I've discovered about life: it's impossible to be frightened and curious at the same time. This is where the third guiding principle, cultivate curiosity, comes in.

PRINCIPLE 3: CULTIVATE CURIOSITY

I ask Loida: how did you become a weaver? Was it something you aspired to, something you wanted to become? The question requires a few iterations as it is translated into T'zutujil. After a few tries, Loida begins talking.

I don't remember exactly when I learned, at what stage of my life, but it was when I was much, much younger. For as long as I can remember, I was surrounded by weavers. I don't ever remember someone sitting down beside me to show me the steps. I just remember that I began weaving and that when I started to weave, I felt sure of myself, like my body knew the steps— how to assemble the threads, how to sit down, which instrument to reach for. "Your hands remember, they know." That's what our grandmothers used to say.

The first step in learning to weave is to develop your curiosity. That drives you to learn, to observe, to listen and to pay attention. Once you have that, the rest just flows. I remember that I had an aunt who dedicated herself to weaving. She made clothes for my grandparents, aunts, and uncles and also sold some of her work. I learned by watching her and other women. I would watch, sometimes ask a question about something they were doing. Then, after a while, I would feel a growing sense of urgency to do something

—to put what I'd been observing into practice and start with my own canvas. The faster I could apply what I was observing, the quicker I learned.

Observing isn't just limited to the actual weaving. You also learn what to weave by observing your surroundings—the patterns of birds, flowers and leaves—these are the patterns we use. Being able to observe your surroundings and translate those patterns into your work, that is what makes a good weaver.

Tendering humility and cultivating curiosity are two attitudes that go hand in hand in *The Weaver's Way*. Humility creates the space wherein we become comfortable with not knowing, and curiosity moves us forward. We learn to lead with questions, not with answers, and value the dialogue that those questions invite.

Curiosity also helps us to move forward from the place of stuckness that we often find ourselves in when dealing with difference. So much of what is happening in the world today is framed into ideologically opposed certainties of right and wrong, good and bad, us versus them. We must be right in a way that makes others wrong. And oftentimes, these polarized dichotomies create false binaries that don't serve us, holding us back from finding new and better solutions.

I am reminded of the well-known Rumi poem that invites us to look beyond our ideas of right and wrong to find each other out in a common field. Curiosity is the force that will guide us to this field, helping us to see that oftentimes, the polarized dichotomies that we use to talk about the world create tensions that don't serve us. Curiosity elevates our perspective. It invites us to imagine a world beyond the binary tradeoffs of a two-option system and to look for a frame of reference that is more expansive and inclusive.

A different field. A different point of view. Even with the same set of circumstances, I have seen time and again how applying curiosity to a situation creates a significantly different outcome. It is a powerful tool for change, which is why a Weaver learns to do so with ease and grace. And one of the key attitudes that helps us learn to do so is guiding principle four.

PRINCIPLE 4: PRACTICE AGILITY AND CONTEXTUAL RESPONSIVENESS

I sit and watch Loida weave amidst the dog-lazing, chicken-scratching, children-tumbling noise and bustle of life unfolding and can't help but smile thinking of my own process when I'm trying to work on a project that feels as complicated and creative as her weaving. For Loida, there's no artist's studio or silent cabin she retreats to in order to concentrate on her work. She weaves amidst the noisy, incessant push of life. The nonstop demands of family, community, and survival mean she is often interrupted. And when she is, she switches with ease from weaver to mother, wife, neighbor, farmer, host. But this ability to move with agility between different identities in response to the context of our surroundings is one that's sorely missing in contemporary Western society.

As we discussed in the previous chapter, we all have many multi-layered identities that make up our whole selves. But the monocultural narratives of the mainstream Western ideology fail to acknowledge or embrace this wonderful richness. Or at least not in a way that allows them to tumble all together.

In his book, *In the Name of Identity*, Lebanese-born French author Amin Maalouf proposes that we all have within us a hierarchy of identities, and when one of those identities is threatened, it rises to the top. He gives the example that when people feel their faith is under attack, their identity with that religious affiliation rises to the top. But if, subsequently, they feel their ethnic group is threatened, then they may find themselves in conflict with their fellow coreligionists[2].

The problem with this idea is it places us at the mercy of external forces, once again forced to don a mask that may not be of our own choosing. It can be an equally powerful act of defiance and resistance to remain dexterous in the face of opposition. We can choose the identities we hold at any particular moment in time. Victim or Survivor. Immigrant or Expat. Or perhaps, None of the Above.

Exploring and becoming comfortable with the plurality of our personalities is just the first step of *The Weaver's Way*'s fourth principle. The next is to learn to be responsive, not reactive, and to develop the ability to move between them with grace and ease like Loida.

Understanding the role of identity and how it influences our work and leadership is important. Just as the Guatemalan weavers move fluidly in and out of weaving as they attend to their other responsibilities, so too does the metaphorical Weaver need to learn agility to move in and out of their own identities, in response to what is happening within and without. Even within the Weaver role itself this duality of identities exists. A Weaver's work is at times that of a craftsman and at times that of an artist. A different set of attitudes and skills is needed for each of these, which is why the Weaver encourages agility and contextual responsiveness.

Note that this idea is very different from the leadership frameworks that try to help you find your strengths or personality traits. While these can be interesting, I have found more often than not they encourage rigidity—once we can characterize ourselves as assertive, relational, visionary, a successor, etc., then those descriptions become part of the narrative we tell ourselves, and it is easy to become locked into our thinking.

As a Weaver, cultivating the agility both in thinking and acting is vital to the success of the work. Rather than finding comfort in a subset of traits, be curious about where you can grow. Embrace the plurality of personalities that makes you uniquely you and bring those to your work of shaping change.

PRINCIPLE 5: EMBRACE TIMEFULLNESS

Time has been one of the biggest areas of exploration, learning, and growth since I first began to think about purposefully shaping change. Back when SERES was starting, it was a significant source of tension between Abigail, Antonio, and myself both at work and in our friendships.

I struggled to understand how they could be constantly late to meetings, then arrive not prepared. I felt frustrated when we worked in communities. Things never started on time, and it always took so long to accomplish tasks that I was certain could be made more efficient with a solid agenda and good facilitation. I was baffled, trying to understand how someone could function in the world when they didn't review their calendar on a regular basis, check their diary, and arrange their schedule around short-, medium-, and long-term priorities. But that was the thing: We were functioning in two very different worlds.

From my so-called professional perspective, time was a linear, quantifiable resource, and I ordered my days around the steady progression of the clock and the calendar. For me, time was also a commodity and therefore efficiency was key. Time was something I spent, and as I spent it, it became scarcer and scarcer. "Time is money," I would say to Abigail. "We need to spend less time on this project." (And do more.)

But Abigail's understanding of time was based on a completely different perspective. Hers was an indigenous worldview that saw time not as linear, but cyclical. In this view of time, things must take their place in a process.

I finally realized exactly how much these two worldviews differed when we overheard a conversation between a couple of foreign tourists sitting behind us one day at a coffee shop. They were talking about observing farmers in the fields "sitting around under the trees, eating and talking."

"If they were so poor," one commented, "surely they would be motivated to work harder so they could make more money."

Feeling a little indignant, I translated the comments for Abigail and asked her what she thought. She seemed hurt but somehow resigned as she told me, "I've heard it many times before. But for us, it's part of the process. I was taught the importance of sharing and eating food on the land that is about to be planted. We eat tortillas before we plant corn or drink a cup of coffee among the coffee trees when we harvest the café. We are investing time, letting the land know what we are doing on it and with it."

Taking this time was an important part of the ritual of planting that kept farmers much more closely connected to their land and each other but was judged as inefficiency or even laziness through a Western lens. The irony was that once Abigail explained, I could see how these traditional practices aligned so much better with the work we were trying to do to help build more sustainable and resilient communities. Where else, I wondered, in my own rush for efficiency and results, had I failed to understand what I was seeing or, worse yet, caused the kind of pain I could see in Abigail's eyes?

I asked Loida more about her relationship with time.

A weaver must learn patience.

To do things in such a way as to not rush someone else or to avoid making your own heart start to shake because something is not happening in the moment or under the circumstances that you need. Everything in nature requires time and the right circumstances to happen. Your job is to be aware of this and learn how to create the right conditions. It is like the farmers. They must wait for the right time for the lifecycle of the corn to be ready to harvest. Rushing the process will not solve anything. Everything has its time.

I listed this as the last of the five guiding principles because for me it was the most difficult to understand and fully appreciate. My entire life, I've been driven by a sense of urgency. That isn't uncommon when we work for issues close to our hearts. But it's also a hallmark of a worldview that commodifies everything and teaches us that our worth is derived from our ability to produce work.

As SERES grew from a grassroots startup into an internationally recognized organization, I found myself emulating those qualities of speed and progress so valued by the dominant leadership archetypes who are the heroes of our mainstream narratives. Whenever there was a problem, I defaulted to action: going into problem-solving mode and immediately trying to fix the problem but not necessarily taking the time to understand the deeper, underlying causes. I rallied our team to be better, faster, stronger behind "the urgency of this moment," and I inspired people with my conviction for the cause. I began to embody that sense of urgency until I was working almost seven days a week and judging other people's commitment by the same standard. It's a clear recipe for burnout.

While I came close many times, my saving grace was that I was surrounded by people who did time differently. That proximity invited me to stop and examine my relationship with time. So I began to explore time through a non-linear, indigenous worldview, thinking about *investing* time rather than *spending* it. Being curious. Paying attention.

As I did, I began to see what operating under the influence of urgency was doing. It was clearly damaging to me. But it was also damaging to my relationships, and ultimately it was undermining the very impact I was hoping to achieve. What I started to see was that when I became driven by a sense of urgency, it was difficult to find the time and space to hear different voices and experiences. Like the farmers in the field or the soft-spoken young women who were intimidated by a strange-sounding foreigner. My need for short-term results was compromising our long-term impact and causing me to default into the old narrative, once again perpetuating the status quo.

The issues I was fighting for were always one of my justifications for the sense of urgency. But as I strove to unlearn urgency, I discovered that this in no way meant losing a sense of importance. In fact as I let go of urgency and the busyness it created, I felt clearer than ever about what was important and where I needed to focus my attention in order to achieve the greatest impact.

To cultivate this sense of patience is to cultivate peace. For those few hours that I'm weaving, I forget about all of my other responsibilities and lose myself in the process. It is a time for reflection and thinking, connecting what's inside with what's outside.

Of course, Loida is not alone in her wisdom. For thousands of years, various spiritual philosophies and religious traditions have extolled the virtues of mindfulness, contemplation, reflection, and patience. The Australian Wiradjuri First Nations people have a concept that captures it well: *Yindyamurra*. Yindyamurra is an expression of profound respect. To do things this way one must be gentle and polite, to honor and do things slowly and with care. This is what I think of when I talk about *timefullness* in *The Weaver's Way* framework. An understanding that the work of shaping change takes time, and our responsibility is to be poised, present, and responsive, sensing into what is required of us at each moment.

As unlearning urgency has been one of my greatest challenges, I developed a small practice to remind me of this sense of timefullness. My desktop screensaver is a photo of one of the beautiful slot canyons in Utah. Whenever I feel the influence of urgency begin to take over—usually in the form of obsessive thoughts or stomach-clenching anxiety—I take a moment to look at that photo and remind myself of the powerful shaping force of water.

Like a Weaver, agile and responsive, water is fluid, soft and yielding. It is guided by its surroundings, sometimes running slow and wide, sometimes deep and strong, and at other times fast and turbulent. But even as it is guided, it never fails to shape, even that which is hard and rigid and cannot yield. This is why we talk about *shaping* change.

These five guiding principles are designed to lead you forward as you begin to think about what it means to be a Weaver and to intentionally engage with the work of shaping change. These guiding principles can apply wherever you are and whatever you're doing. Whether you're at your child's soccer match, trying to create change in your organization, or trying to make your community a better place.

As Loida weaves she enters a state of flow, becoming present to the rhythm of weaving itself as well as the rhythm of whatever is happening around her. She's not thinking of the Guiding Principles. They are simply a part of her and her work. That's what we aim for as Weavers, to become so familiar with these principles they become second nature, and it becomes difficult to think of *not* responding to the world in this way. That's exactly how it is for Therese, whom I'd like you to meet.

WEAVER: THERESE CAOUETTE

I first met Therese in 2019 when she was visiting Guatemala helping guide a donor interested in funding organizations supporting women and girls. She'd contacted me through a mutual friend, wondering if I could introduce her to different local leaders and organizations so they could get a better understanding of the landscape.

From the outset, Therese was clear: They would be providing compensation for any local leaders who gave their time to meet with her, and they were committed to providing funding for any organization included as part of their initial research. She recognized the kinds of time and resources required for organizations to meet with people interested in learning about their work and understood this took away from important mission-related work.

It was the first time in ten years that I'd met someone from the funding side like Therese, who clearly had a deep appreciation of the value of local knowledge and an acute awareness of the power dynamics so common in most funding relationships. I was curious to learn more about her story, and with a five-day trip across Guatemala, I had a wonderful opportunity to do so.

As I came down to breakfast the next morning, Therese was speaking into her mobile phone in a language I couldn't place. After she was done, I asked her what it was. "Thai," she told me, then pointed at her phone. "These smart phones have been a game changer for our work in so many ways." Such as being able to send voice notes back and forth to people in her network who speak Thai but don't know how to read or write it. That's a common scenario among migrant and refugee communities in Southeast Asia, she tells me.

Intrigued, I asked her more about what that work is, and she tells me about a number of different initiatives: supporting undocumented ethnic minorities to access social services, getting education to migrant factory workers' children, mobile financing for "unbankable" ethnic minority groups.

True to Weaver form, there is no "I" in these stories. She can talk for hours, but rarely does Therese talk about her own role. Instead, she is constantly lifting up and celebrating the achievements of the local leaders who are driving forward these efforts.

Later that day making small talk on a six-hour drive into the highlands of Quiché, I ask Therese what she will be doing after this trip. "Going to Davos," she says with a half smile. "My husband's invited, and I go with him."

She is talking about the World Economic Forum, an annual event for the world's richest and most powerful people. In the space of a month, Therese can be cycling up along the mountainous Thai-Burma border, heading to a meeting with women's justice advocates in Guatemala, then sitting at dinner sharing a glass of wine with a tech billionaire. And she does so with agility and flexibility, without guile or pretense, moving in and out of her different roles as she leverages her privileges for the change she is so passionate about.

Therese understands deeply what it takes to shape meaningful, transformative change because she has spent over thirty-five years—more than half of her life—doing it, fighting for the rights of some of the world's most isolated and marginalized populations in the Mekong region of Southeast Asia.

Yet despite having impacted the lives of hundreds of thousands of people, and contributing toward significant systemic and structural changes, it is difficult to keep Therese in the spotlight for long. In true Weaver style, Therese is wary of a hero story. "By making people into heroes," says Therese, "it frees individuals of our responsibility to take action." She also acknowledges that it is important to tell stories but insists that these stories come from what she describes as a vulnerable, humble space, the kind of space that makes you one of the people, not above the people.

"There's nothing special about me," insists Therese, "I just stayed engaged in the world, saw injustice, and acted on it. And that's what we need people, everyone, to do."

I agree with Therese on almost everything except one small point—that there's nothing special about her. Because more than anyone else I've come across, Therese embodies the five guiding principles of *The Weaver's*

Way, and she has used these principles to guide a lifetime of shaping change.

As is often the case, Therese found her place in the world through a circuitous route. She grew up in the United States in the Midwest during the time of segregation, and neither her school nor her community offered much in the way of diversity. That is, until the end of the Vietnam War, when her town became a hub for Southeast Asian refugees. Suddenly, Therese found herself learning beside and later working with students and families whose lives and stories were vastly different from her own. She developed new friendships, along with a curiosity about working across cultures. After graduating college, that curiosity led her to Southeast Asia where she spent the next ten years working with refugees and displaced persons in emergency relief operations.

You may recall that the Weaver's Journey of Becoming asks us to be willing to put ourselves in uncomfortable situations and there, to bear witness to injustice and risk the pain of a broken heart, all while staying open and engaged with the world around us. This is something that Therese is no stranger to.

She shares a story about a time in the 1980s, following the fall of the Khmer Rouge and its brutal regime when she'd been working in a refugee camp on the Cambodian border. The camp contained approximately 160,000 people squeezed into two square miles. Therese was working with a team of about 200 people: a small group of international relief staff supported by refugees from the camp itself, who were responsible for organizing food distribution, basic health services, and primary education.

Then one morning, the noise and bustle of humanity crowded in upon itself was suddenly replaced by the deafening thuds of mortars being dropped from on high. The camp was being shelled. A Situation 4 came over the walkie-talkie that Therese was required to carry at all times when in the camp: immediate evacuation of all international staff. And so, amidst the deafening thuds and deadly silences, Therese and her international colleagues climbed into the vehicles and joined the convoy racing out of the camp.

"It was a terrible sick feeling," says Therese, "staring back through the dust clouds at the faces of colleagues and friends, knowing they were trapped in a place under attack. I wish I could say unequivocally that I stood with those refugees in a time of need. But what is the opposite of standing with your fellow human? Driving away."

Therese goes on to explain how for her, the freedom of leaving that camp came with a lifelong responsibility. "Driving out didn't mean I got to go home. It meant I had to live with it. I realized I had to do more than my job. I had to use my privilege to listen, and to speak out on behalf of those who couldn't. I had to know deep down that I was doing whatever I could. I had to live each day of my life with deep discomfort, and deep respect."

Therese has learned to live with discomfort, which has made her more adept at living with the paradoxical tension of having access to spaces of enormous power and privilege, as well as those without. "Being prepared to be uncomfortable, to not have to resolve that discomfort with an easy answer, is so important," says Therese. But she also acknowledges it isn't something that comes easily to people. As an adjunct professor at Thammasat University in Bangkok, it is something she attempts with varying degrees of success to teach her students. Therese tries to get her students to lead with a question, not an answer, and learn to hold the space of dialectic tension that requires acknowledging complex trade-offs instead of searching for simple solutions.

"But when your education system tells you that to succeed you need to get A's, and to get A's you need to have the right answer, it's challenging for students to think differently," she says. "We aren't taught to sit in discomfort. But you can't go out into the world and hope to create meaningful change with a bunch of A's."

Part of the problem, notes Therese, is the erroneous idea this work is linear. In her teaching, she uses the business concept of Real Time Strategy to get her students more comfortable with the idea of emergence. "I try to get them to understand that the way we need to work involves being in the moment, moving with the players, understanding the dynamics, seeing the things happening on the ground," says Therese. "It is multifaceted in multiple dimensions—you can't capture that on a Gantt chart or a log frame."

I ask Therese to tell me a little more about how this approach has played out in her work.

"One of the great things about it," she tells me, "is that you discover a different rhythm, a different way of working." When you are no longer constantly beholden to externally imposed drivers, you become more responsive to what is happening around you. You create the space for serendipity. You invest time. "Ultimately," says Therese, "that's what it takes to build trust." And trust is essential for shaping meaningful and transformative change.

Therese shares with me another story, about a time in 1988 when the military crackdown in Myanmar forced many young students and activists across the border into Thailand. As she worked to help the Burmese students organize and support those fleeing, she began to notice another trend: a steady increase in young girls, picked up at the border and funneled into enslavement as sex workers or other abusive and degrading work.

Therese began lobbying international human rights groups to bring their attention to the plight of these young girls, who eventually responded by asking her to investigate and document the abuses: in six weeks. "The idea was ludicrous," says Therese. "To think that you could go to anyone suffering a human rights violation and just expect them to open up and tell their story."

So Therese took a six-month leave, and told the organization that she would deliver the report when she got back. She spent that time hanging out in the market, eating noodles at the shops, getting to know people and building relationships. "We spent five months just being in that space," she explains, "and we probably got all of the interviews and data in the last two weeks. You have to invest time and trust before you can do anything substantial, anything that will last beyond you and have an impact beyond the project itself."

I ask Therese now, toward the end of her career, what thoughts she has, looking back. "It's funny," she says, "I don't think of my career, because for me, this was never really a job. It's a lifestyle. It's not about being in a certain place or having a certain position. Wherever you are, that's where you do it: Be present, listen, engage with change. Right where you are. You can do it as a mother, as a bank teller, as a soccer coach. It's a way of respecting, listening, having curiosity about each other, engaging with each other, and creating the spaces where change is possible."

SUMMARY

- *The Weaver's Way* outlines five guiding principles that help us to think about how to approach the work of Weaving.
- The five guiding principles invite us to use tension as a source of creativity and innovation, work with humility, cultivate curiosity, embrace the diversity within and between us, be agile and responsive, and embrace a non-linear version of time.
- As we become more adept at using these guiding principles, we become more poised and present, and better equipped to respond to the world with care and compassion.

EXERCISES

1. TENSION AS A TOOL.
How do you use tension at home? At work? Does it feel constructive or destructive? The three scenarios below briefly describe the three common ways of dealing with tension, or conflict. Which of these is most familiar to you?

- Pursuing conflict (destructive): adversarial, hostile, attacking/defensive, feels like a battle zone, combative language, win for self, controlling, self-interest only, rigid/reactive.
- Avoiding conflict (destructive): protective, avoid losing, "survival" mode, self-interest only, feels difficult to engage, passive-aggressive, withholding, manipulating.
- Using tension (constructive): trust-based, mutual gain, cooperative, connected, curious, engaging, open to influence, supportive.

In the first two scenarios, the conflictive situation rarely leads to creative and innovative outcomes.

While you can't control others' reactions, maintaining a non-defensive presence in the face of conflicts and disagreements and facilitating conversations that allow space for vulnerability and openness can greatly contribute toward creating an environment that is more collaborative and supportive. Try it next time you notice a conflict emerging and see if you can learn to dance with tension!

2. PRACTICE IDENTITY YOGA.
As Maalouf explains, external settings and circumstances often influence which of our identities rises to the surface. Identity yoga is about being agile in your identities, learning to be responsive instead of reactive, and claiming the power to choose which of our identities shows up and why.

Notice if there are situations in your life where one particular identity is dominant. Why do you think that happens? Is there room for choice? What would happen if some of your other, less visible, identities were present?

3. ENGAGE WITH CHANGE WHEREVER YOU ARE.

As Therese tells us, shaping change is not a job but a lifestyle. "Wherever you are, that's where you do it: Be present, listen, engage with change. Right where you are. You can do it as a mother, as a bank teller, as a soccer coach. It's a way of respecting, listening, having curiosity about each other, engaging with each other, and creating the spaces where change is possible."

Think about the different spaces that you occupy. Each of these spaces are opportunities for shaping change. How does Therese's guidance help you to think about shaping change in those spaces?

CHAPTER 6

THE LAWS OF
INTERCONNECTEDNESS

> " Without inner change there can be no outer change,
> without collective change, no change matters.

— ANGEL KYODO WILLIAMS

In Chapter 5, we discussed *The Weaver's Way* framework as having two distinct but interconnected elements: the *Weaver* as an identity, someone who shapes change, and *Weaving* as the way that change is shaped. In this chapter, we focus on the first of those two concepts and discuss what it takes to *become* the Weaver.

This work of *becoming* is vital. Although cliché, Gandhi's much quoted "We must become the change we wish to see in the world" is as pertinent today as ever. We cannot do the work of trying to change and transform the world unless we are willing to change and transform ourselves. Why not?

The Weaver's Way Framework

THE LAWS OF INTERCONNECTEDNESS

Just as an engineer's work is governed by the laws of the physical world, a Weaver's work must respect at all times the Laws of Interconnectedness.

Each and everyone's existence is deeply tied to that of others. We are at a pivotal moment in human history, facing challenges too profound and complex to be overcome by any single person, government, or nation. Successfully overcoming these challenges will be determined in large part by our ability to restore our connections to ourselves, to each other, and to the earth to a healthy state. To become a Weaver, therefore, we must understand what it truly means to live in an interconnected world.

THE WORLD THROUGH UBUNTU

While interconnectedness is an idea that's just making its way into Western thinking, it's a concept that's embedded into the foundations of indigenous knowledge from many different cultures around the world. Ubuntu is probably the most well-recognized version of this. An African concept, Ubuntu has managed to transcend culture all the way from its Zulu and Xhosa roots to the stratospheric level of social media memes and hashtags.

Yet in gaining those heights, this indigenous worldview has been reduced to nothing more than a promotional tool for the humanity *lite* version of connectedness that's a hallmark of globalization. *I am because you are,* says the meme written across the top of a photo of some bare-footed brown children sitting in a circle. But do we truly appreciate the meaning of these words?

The indigenous wisdom embodied in Ubuntu and other similar concepts of relationality encompassed within indigenous cultural domains goes far beyond a simplistic idea of oneness. It speaks to a worldview that deeply understands and embraces the consequences of interconnectedness. Ubuntu tells us that "I am because we are, and since we are, therefore I am."

Aileen Moreton-Robinson, an Australian author, academic and member of the Goenpul tribe, Quandamooka First Nations, explains how this idea of relationality is expressed. "A person experiences the self as part of others and that others are part of self," she writes in her book, *Talkin' up to the White Woman: Indigenous Women and Feminism*. It is a concept taught in Australian First Nations culture "through reciprocity, obligation, shared experiences, coexistence, cooperation, and social memory."[1]

"A person with Ubuntu," writes Archbishop Desmond Tutu in his book *No Future Without Forgiveness*, "is open and available to others, affirming of others, does not feel threatened that others are able and good, for he or she has a proper self-assurance that comes from knowing that he or she belongs in a greater whole."[2] I can't help but wonder, as I scroll through the 1.1 million #Ubuntu Instagram posts—mainly of beautiful people in pristine places—if the two concepts could get any further apart.

In one of my conversations with Loida I asked her to tell me, in her own words, what weaving meant to her. "Weaving is freedom, expression, wisdom, salvation," she told me. Loida and I had explored the ideas of freedom, expression, and wisdom in much of what we'd already discussed about literal and metaphorical weaving. But weaving for salvation? The idea was provocative, and it has stayed with me, tucked away in the back of my mind.

Then one day as I was working on rewriting a leadership curriculum I'd developed when SERES was in its infancy, I came across a quote from Dr. Lilla Watson I'd included in the introduction to the curriculum:

"If you have come to help me, you are wasting your time. If you have come because your liberation is bound up with mine, then let us work together."

Dr. Watson is an Australian First Nations Aboriginal Murri elder, activist, and educator from Gangulu country in North Eastern Queensland. This idea of shared liberation was first expressed by an aboriginal rights group that Watson was working with out of frustration at white Australians' continued framing of the consequences of a racist, colonial system as *trying to fix an aboriginal problem*. What Watson and so many other social justice advocates since her were asking for was a recognition of interconnectedness, or Ubuntu.

In working with the Laws of Interconnectedness, the Weaver understands they are part of a greater system and that when one part of the system suffers, all parts are affected. In Archbishop Tutu's words, "(we are) diminished when others are humiliated or diminished, when others are tortured or oppressed, or treated as if they were less than who they are."[3] In other words when a Weaver works to shape change, it isn't about trying to help or save the other. When we work for change, we work for our shared liberation. We weave for our salvation.

One of the consequences of the old individualist narrative is that it reinforces an erroneous idea of separateness. But if we hope to shape meaningful and transformative change, we must shift this perspective and ground our work and approach in a deep understanding and acceptance of interconnectedness. Let's take a moment to examine this idea through an example that most people will be familiar with: the traditional philanthropic charity model.

LEANING DOWN OR LEANING IN?

I remember being in a leadership seminar some years back with social change leaders from around the world when one of my colleagues shared a quote: "The American policies of termination and extermination weren't as detrimental to American Indians as the goodwill of white women."

At the time we were exploring the delicate realm of race, power, and privilege. I could see how this statement could make some people, a white woman like me, for example, feel defensive. Yet at the same time I knew there was a message here that was important for us as a group to understand.

Her words reminded me of a TED talk I'd just watched by His Holiness Pope Francis titled "Why the only future worth building includes everyone," and one particular line that stood out to me. "Good intentions and conventional formulas, so often used to appease our conscience, are not enough," he warned the audience. "We must remember that the other is not a statistic, or a number...we all need each other."[4] Could it be, I asked the group, that what our colleague and Pope Francis were inviting us to consider were the Laws of Interconnectedness?

While well-intentioned, many of our charitable endeavors have historically been rooted in separateness, the attitude that so frustrated Watson and her colleagues back in the 1970s and that undoubtedly was the root of the comment about the goodwill of white women. Separateness draws a line between "us" and "them" and, if not checked, can lead to the kinds of conditions in which a harmful combination of power and pity flourishes.

As American theologian Reinhold Niebuhr explores, writing in 1930s USA in his book *Moral Man and an Immoral Society*, a person's donation to charity was a "display of his power and an expression of his pity," and that "his generous impulse freezes within him if his power is challenged or his generosities are accepted without suitable humility."[5]

In Part I we discussed the importance of stories and the effects that labels within those stories can have on how we think about ourselves and others. In this story of separateness, one character takes the role of the charitable savior and hence requires the other to play the victim. Which, according to Niebuhr, explains why those who benefit from the mainstream narrative are more inclined to be generous than to grant social justice.

This idea of separateness continues to permeate throughout many of our stories about change. Let's consider a very real and complex twenty-first century problem, what is often referred to as the refugee crisis. To illustrate, I'd like to introduce you to a friend of mine, Haile Kassa. While most of the stories that I share in this book are about people who are doing the work of shaping change, Haile's story, at least in the beginning, is a little different. His is the story of the recipient, someone whom society decided needed to be changed, and the experience of being "the other."

WEAVER: HAILE KASSA

I first met Haile in 2018, ten years after he fled Ethiopia with plans to claim asylum in Switzerland. Haile prefers not to be identified as belonging to a particular ethnic group, but back in Ethiopia that identity, foisted upon him, was very much a part of determining his rights, his survival, his future. At twenty-four years of age, Haile decided to leave his home and his family in the hopes of finding a way that he could freely contribute to society without constant fear of persecution or reprisal.

When it comes to the old narrative for shaping change, the plight of the recipient is one that has never wanted for narrators. But rarely are the narrators the recipients themselves. This is certainly the case for refugees, and when I reached out to Haile to ask if he would share his story with me, I could tell that he was moved by the invitation. In Haile's words, being asked to share his story, to talk about who he is, is a huge honor. I suspect that in large part this is because he was denied his own story for such a long time.

"The moment I arrived," explains Haile, "I was put into a box and labeled a refugee. Who I was, what I was capable of—none of that mattered to anyone." The experience as he described it was akin to being wiped clean of your past. You're allowed one carefully crafted and curated story, molded by those whose job it is to move you through the asylum claim process. But even that story, edited and re-edited to fit someone else's version of appropriateness, no longer feels like your own.

For more than half of the ten years he'd been in Switzerland, Haile had lived as a refugee in six different camps, transferred back and forth between them as he waited to be processed. And waiting, it seemed, was all he was supposed to do. As a refugee, it quickly became obvious to Haile that he was expected to behave and act in a certain way. In order for the system to work, it required homogeneity. "I was only allowed to be a refugee, nothing else. I could learn German, but only to a certain level. I could leave the camp, but only go a certain distance."

Initiative and innovation were discouraged, and to Haile it felt that every way he turned he was restricted from giving his best, being his best. "One of the saddest things," he explains to me, "is that I knew people were investing resources in us—money, food, shelter, language training. But I never felt it came from a place of genuine care. I always felt I was nothing more than just a piece of work for some social worker."

In this traditional approach to shaping change, Haile was a problem that had to be solved. "The last thing I ever expected was to come to Switzerland and sit around idly, but that was the reality. It was the most disempowering experience." And he could see that it wasn't just disempowering to those who were refugees but to many of the case workers involved. "I knew that some of them at least did want to help me. I could see their frustration. But they could only do what the system let them do." After two years of waiting, Haile—frustrated by inactivity and feeling at his wit's end—knew he had to find something to do. While he wasn't permitted to work, no one mentioned study, and Haile knew that the University would review his case regardless of the fact that he was a refugee. He applied for, and was accepted into, a master's program.

Then came the next hurdle—how to pay for the program. Haile himself had no money, and even if he found a scholarship or sponsorship, he was told that his status as a refugee wouldn't allow him to accept it. After fruitlessly arguing his case all the way up to the person responsible for the canton, who was the final authority on the rights of refugees in his area, Haile was told by a case worker if you do find a way, we can't know about it.

To Haile that statement offered a sliver of hope, and with only a week until the program started, he went door-to-door to over twenty NGOs looking for someone who might be able to support him. After countless rejections, he finally found it. Someone willing to cover his tuition. Haile was thrilled. After over twenty-four months of doing nothing, he finally had the opportunity for meaningful engagement. "This meant much more to me than being able to study," Haile explains. "It was about finally having agency, meaning, connection."

And yet even this achievement was bittersweet because his accomplishment had to remain a secret. While it seemed impossible to him, Haile was still invisible.

Haile graduated from the master's program, and after waiting another year for his status to be granted, he was finally able to begin working. "I always believed that once I got permission to work, things would be easy," he told me. But he was wrong once again. "I applied for hundreds of jobs, and all I got was hundreds of rejections." Once again, Haile felt stuck, unable to move forward, no matter how hard he tried.

Then one day, after being told once again that the solution to his problem was integration, Haile had a realization. He was still living the same story he'd been living in the camps for over six years because after so long, Haile had begun to see himself as "the other." "Everyone was constantly telling me that in order to get a job, I needed to integrate," he told me.

But, Haile realized, integration was the storyline for refugees. "The refugee experience is such a disempowering experience," he told me, and not for the first time. It was obvious he wanted me to understand this. "You're made to feel smaller and smaller, to feel more and more powerless until suddenly, you start believing it." If he wanted to change, Haile realized, he had to escape the narrative that always required him to be powerless. He had to stop being the other. "I suddenly realized I didn't want to integrate like a refugee," he says. "I wanted to belong."

Haile didn't want to be processed as another anonymous number. He wanted to be seen as a person, one who had something to give to the society that was supporting him. To do so, Haile had to erase the boundaries of difference that had been created by the us/them story of separation.

This realization was the beginning of an important shift.

Haile was ready to take back ownership of his story. But, he realized, he needed to start with himself. In order to belong he had to begin to address his own feelings of fear, mistrust, and separateness that had arisen after so many years of being invisible. So he did.

"I realized that complaining was destroying me, and blaming wasn't going to get me anywhere. I didn't want to tell myself after thirty or forty years of my life, looking back, that I had never belonged. I wasn't ready to live like that. I wanted to feel at home. To do that, I had to understand what feeling at home felt like here, in Switzerland. So I got curious." Driven by this deep desire for belonging, he began asking: What does it mean to belong here in this place, with these people?

And that inquiry, those questions, he told me with a small laugh, took him to the places he had so deeply longed for. Places like the leadership program where we met in 2018.

"So tell me," I asked, "what was the difference?" It was obvious Haile had thought about this a lot, and his answer came quickly. "It's unconditional love."

I'd never thought about the old narrative for shaping change through this lens, but as I listened to Haile talk, it made sense to me. Conditional love was how Haile described his experience as a refugee and is something to which he has become finely attuned.

Such as when an individual or institution is trying to help a person or population that's worse off. The giving/receiving relationship, he explained, is dominated by conditional love. And the receiving end doesn't flourish because the support is always given conditionally, which becomes a form of control. "Looking at it now from a neutral perspective," explained Haile, "it seems almost nonsensical, that the system would be designed to disempower, rather than help people to pursue their purpose. But I realize now that it has to do with fear and power."

They are two ideas that show up a lot in our old change narrative. "Unconditional love," Haile explained, "is free from fear and control." And that is what he experienced when he started coming to the workshops and events like the one where we met.

For the first time in many years, Haile found himself fully accepted, just as he was. "I didn't have to be or act a certain way, tell my story a certain way. I wasn't afraid of being judged or evaluated," he said, a feeling which he described as "unconditional love in action."

I asked Haile to tell me what was the most significant change as a result of these two very different experiences. "I got my own power back," he explained, "and that has changed my entire journey. My environment feeds me. I feel accepted, welcome, and that creates a positive feedback loop to keep working for change. I still don't know what the future holds, what to expect, but I'm okay with that uncertainty."

Unconditional love in action gave Haile access to spaces where he was free to choose who he wanted to be, and the story line he wanted to follow. Which in his case is now helping to replicate his own liberating transformation with other people facing a similar situation.

Haile calls it unconditional love. I call it solidarity. But whatever you call it, the meaning is the same. It's about working from a foundation of common liberation and shared salvation, from the understanding that we belong together and we need each other.

As I listen to Haile speak, I'm reminded of a quote by Uruguayan journalist Eduardo Galeano. "I don't believe in charity. I believe in solidarity," says Galeano. "Charity is so vertical. It goes from the top to the bottom. Solidarity is horizontal. It respects the other person. I have a lot to learn from other people."[6]

WHAT DO WE HAVE TO LEARN FROM HAILE, AND OTHERS LIKE HIM? PLENTY IT turns out.

This idea of erasing the boundaries of difference, of practicing unconditional love in action, is all about the horizontal work of solidarity. Charity asks us to lean down and help the other. Solidarity invites us to lean in and help ourselves. And when a community learns to lean in, it is much more likely to fall together than fracture apart during times of upheaval and crisis.

What does a horizontal approach working with refugees look like? Let's ask Haile. After reclaiming ownership of his own story, he looked for ways to help others do the same.

"I wanted to design a way to take other people, other refugees on a journey of owning their experience," he explained. "To help them to understand the obstacles aren't just outside, they are also inside." Haile's goal was to free them from the story they'd been handed when they were first labeled refugees and to help them choose a new narrative. "Because no matter how powerless you feel, that is one thing you always have power over."

He volunteered for a program for communities of Ethiopian and Sudanese youth but quickly noticed a gap. The programs offered had all been designed by people who came from a completely different context. If the programs were going to be effective, they needed to be designed by people who understood the refugee's own context. They needed to be designed by refugees themselves.

Through his own advocacy, Haile got involved with designing curriculum for young refugees. "We took what was meant to be a job training program, and we focused on helping participants design their own change journey. We helped them value their own wisdom and see their incredible journeys of survival as strengths. Yeah...they come to find a job." He nodded. "But more importantly? They rediscover themselves!"

Haile's goal now, working with the United Nations Refugee Agency UNHCR, is to try to institutionalize this approach and find a systemic way to help people realize their own potential. "Unconditional love," said Haile, "is a difficult thing for the mainstream narrative to understand. But I'm trying."

Haile's work shows how fundamental it is to shape change within the Laws of Interconnectedness, grounding our work in unconditional love and solidarity. "The future of humankind," the Pope said in the concluding remarks of his TED talk, "is in the hands of those people who recognize the other as a 'you' and themselves as part of an 'us.'"[7]

In other words, the future is in the hands of Weavers.

SUMMARY

- The Laws of Interconnectedness are an expression of the idea that each and everyone's existence is deeply tied to that of others. When one part of the system suffers, all parts are affected.
- A Weaver's work is deeply grounded in the concept of Interconnectedness—eliminating the idea of "us" and "them." In Weaving, there is no "other."
- Weaving is a horizontal rather than top-down process. By leaning in and embracing a sense of solidarity with those who we want to support, we create stronger social ties and connections which are essential for building resilience.

EXERCISES

1. CONNECT WITH THE OTHER

Identify someone you interact with on a regular basis, but don't engage with. Someone you identify as "other." They may be "other" because they have a different political viewpoint or come from a different socio-economic group. Perhaps they have a different race, ethnicity, or religion.

What assumptions do you make about this person? How do those assumptions influence the way you interact or engage?
Next, spend some time thinking not about the ways that you are different, but about what things you may have in common. Under what circumstances might you share the same joy or sorrow? Keep this in mind the next time you meet, and allow it to guide your interaction.

2. TRUST AND OTHERNESS

Haile's story demonstrated how the feeling of otherness can undermine trust which in turn can detract from creating real change. Take a moment to think about the people who might be impacted by the changes you want to bring about—especially if they represent groups that are different in some way. Now, imagine a linear scale from 1-10 with one representing a total stranger and ten representing the people that you most trust in this world. Where do these people you are hoping to work with currently sit on the scale?

Building trust takes time, intimacy, breaking down the distinctions of otherness and building up our shared similarities. And it is different for everyone. Take a moment to reflect on what it would take to move this relationship up the scale of trust—for you, and for them.

CHAPTER 7
THE JOURNEY OF BECOMING

 We need to discern who we are and expand on our humanness and sacredness. That's how we change the world, which happens because WE will be the change.

— DR. GRACE LEE BOGGS

O nce ready to acknowledge and accept the Laws of Interconnectedness, the Journey of Becoming can begin. But I want to be honest with you. The journey you're about to undertake will be at times confronting. You'll be asked to face uncomfortable truths and difficult questions and accept that you may not have all of the answers.

It's a hard but necessary part of the journey of becoming a Weaver.

FINDING YOUR WAY HOME

Just as the literal weaver accepts the discomfort of kneeling for hours on the hard dirt floor, so too does a skillful Weaver understand that part of the journey is to get comfortable with being uncomfortable. In the words of Bryan Stevenson, a death row attorney and founder of the Equal Justice Initiative, "There is no path to justice that is only comfortable and convenient. We will not create justice until we're willing to sometimes position ourselves in uncomfortable places and be a witness."[1]

The Journey of Becoming asks us to stand with our eyes wide open, opening ourselves up to the painful reality of a world in distress. It asks us not to numb ourselves and turn away, but to instead turn toward, to embrace that which may harm, hurt or ail us. It's a journey that undoubtedly requires courage, bravery, and sacrifice. But don't let that discourage you. Because it's also a journey that holds a promise.

Becoming a Weaver is an invitation to open your eyes and see —*truly* see—the world you are living in. This may seem simple. But simplicity should not be mistaken for triviality. Indeed, this may be one of the bravest things you've ever done.

To open our eyes and see, we must learn to pay attention. It's no easy task. In fact, it's quite possible you've spent your entire adult life doing just the opposite. In today's noisy world, it's not only an exercise in discipline and concentration but also an act of extreme courage. To live with eyes wide open, to be aware of what is happening to the planet and her people, is to risk living with a broken heart every day. Our natural tendency is to avoid that which is painful or uncomfortable. Thus, as we become adults, we teach ourselves to look away and *stop* paying attention. We disengage and numb ourselves to the world around us. But to what end?

Psychologists and researchers the world over have demonstrated it is neither healthy nor productive to avoid unpleasant emotions. As renowned author and research professor Dr. Brené Brown writes in her book, *Dare to Lead*, "We cannot selectively numb emotion. If we numb the dark, we numb the light. If we take the edge off pain and discomfort, we are, by default, taking the edge off joy, love, belonging, and the other emotions that give meaning to our lives."[2] Brown urges her readers and followers to lean in to discomfort, claiming this is the way not only to rise above the pain, but to renew our spirit as we do so.

This makes me think about one of my favorite poets, Mary Oliver, and her poem "Sometimes," in which she gives her readers advice for living a good life. *Pay attention* is her first instruction. Can we skip Mary's sage council and still live a full and meaningful life? I believe both Mary and Brené would agree.

We cannot.

When we blind ourselves to the world around us, when we numb ourselves to the pain, we also stop living our own lives and surrender ourselves to the Game—unwitting players governed by invisible rules, never quite sure if we're the winners or losers.

So here's the promise.

The Journey of Becoming is a journey of discovery. You will learn new ways of being in the world. You will forge stronger relationships and more authentic connections. You will find new sources of hope and inspiration. You will uncover a deeper sense of meaning and worth for your life and your life's work. This will be your journey home.

TO SACRIFICE IGNORANCE

To begin to shape meaningful change a Weaver must learn to pay attention. But paying attention isn't just an act of courage. It's one of sacrifice as well. Because in order to pay attention, we must give up the gift of ignorance. And ignorance, as they say, is bliss!

Ignorance is often defined as a lack of knowledge or education. I disagree. Or at least, I believe that it's more nuanced. Ignorance is derived from our privileges, which shelter us from discomfort and protect us from inconvenient truths. It's both ironic and paradoxical. Ironic in that it's usually our privilege that gives us access to things like education. Paradoxical in that, in the words of Darren Walker, CEO of the Ford Foundation, "It shields us from fully experiencing or acknowledging inequality, even while giving us more power to do something about it."[3]

This is the journey of becoming a Weaver which is as much about looking back as it is about moving forward. Our stories are part of a continuum, the larger tapestry that makes up the human story. Understanding our place in this continuum opens us up to the possibility of change. If we are focused only on the here and now, without this deeper sense of time, we can easily believe that who we are now is who we've always been. In that state, change may indeed feel impossible, or at least improbable. As we locate ourselves on this historical throughline, we open up to the possibility of a different future.

As you begin the journey, you may be required to examine difficult truths about the world and your place in it. And to accept that your own story may be implicated in uncomfortable narratives. Doing this takes courage, bravery, and sacrifice and a willingness to get uncomfortable. And someone who I've witnessed do that time and again is Patty Curran.

WEAVER: PATTY CURRAN

After living and working in Southeast Asia for twenty-five years Patty, in her midfifties, made the decision to move herself and her family back to her hometown of South Bend, Indiana, and in March 2020 started a new job as the Executive Director of Partners Asia—an organization for which she'd served on the board for a number of years. Needless to say, it was a tough time to be starting a new job—especially a nonprofit, which relied on the generous donations and support of people whose own lives had suddenly become so much more precarious.

Partners Asia is in itself an unusual organization. For over twenty years, they've been working with local community partners in Southeast Asia, pursuing an approach that flips the script on traditional power dynamics and places the needs and desires of local leaders and local organizations first. In a field where external forces dictate which community problems receive recognition, which solutions will be supported (regardless of whether these approaches are prioritized by the people who live there), and where foreign actors and international agencies have continuously overshadowed local voices, Partners Asia's alternative way of working is a Weaver approach through and through.

But that's not the reason I've included Patty's story here.

The international development space is one which has unashamedly perpetuated the old narrative, often seeming to serve almost as a "last mile" delivery solution for the patterns of patriarchy, colonization, and extractivism by promoting them into the hardest to reach communities and among the most disenfranchised and impoverished populations. And while Partners Asia had been successfully following an alternative model for many years, it had done so quietly, with a trusted group of local partners and donors.

But with the world-shifting events of a global pandemic and international uprising for racial justice as her induction, Patty took a look at the field that she was now working in and decided that the time for being quiet was over.

Patty is one of a small but rapidly growing group of development professionals determined to change the way development and philanthropy work. She believes it's time the sector faced some difficult questions. "To what extent does conventional development practice reflect exported systemic racism and structural inequalities? What power imbalances get perpetuated in the way we build partnerships, structure agreements, or give funding? What types of biases exist for deciding whose voice gets heard?" she asks.

For twenty-five years while living in Southeast Asia, Patty saw time and again how the colonization of aid had too often been an ineffective, inefficient, and disempowering practice that stifled the abilities, insights, and expertise of local changemakers. "By not facing these questions, by not identifying and resourcing organizations and leaders who truly serve their communities," explained Patty, "we have seen the perpetuation of the very problems that large international NGOs have tried to eliminate."

But here is where Patty's courage and bravery come in.

Patty could easily have continued quietly with Partners Asia, doing great work supported by a loyal community of donors. But by putting herself out there, by asking these questions, she is opening herself up to the very same criticism.

There are people who would look at her organization, see a white woman from North America at the helm, and call her a hypocrite. She told me about a recent interaction with a foundation representative who told her point blank: "We'd rather fund organizations that don't have executive directors who look like you."

Patty knows facing these uncomfortable truths is part of the journey, and she isn't afraid. She recognizes that being able to engage in these kinds of difficult discussions, ones for which there are no readily available answers, is what it takes to shape change. But one thing isn't negotiable. "The thing about the 'people who look like me' position," Patty observed, "is that it is a perpetuation of 'us' and 'them.' This isn't just about changing who sits at the top or who has the power. That's the old story. This is about writing a whole new story."

As long as she's doing that, the discomfort's worth it.

BUILDING BRIDGES

Where does this determination—this ability to show up each day and challenge the status quo through myriad daily acts of love, courage, passion, and commitment—come from? I've seen Patty work, and I know the answer. It's relationships.

Relationships are the cornerstone of Patty's work. But they aren't just any relationships.

I mentioned at the beginning of Part II that *The Weaver's Way* framework is one focused on building community bridges rather than tribal bonds. This is an important distinction. Bonding networks are ones in which I relate to people who look like me, talk like me, and think like me. In those kinds of networks, everyone else is alien or foreign or scary.

Bridging networks, on the other hand, create a sense of belonging with people who may look and sound different but who share the same beliefs or values. They are connections woven from our common humanity, and the relationships formed through these bridging networks are vital to the work of Weaving.

Patty's relationships with people on the frontlines—people such as human rights advocates, undocumented migrants, or LGBTQI activists—are bridges built on trust, dignity, and respect. She understands that change that is relational—crafted through conversation, connection, and collaboration—is transformational.

Life is about interactions. It flows through our relations and our relationships, crafting our realities and understanding of the world. By building authentic relationships between diverse groups of people, Weavers like Patty help to nourish our capacity for connection and caring in an increasingly divided world. As Tehranian poet Kamand Kojouri writes in her poem "They Want Us to Be Afraid":

> They are so ignorant they don't understand
> that my soul and your soul are old friends.
> They are so ignorant they don't understand
> that when they cut you, I bleed.

As long as she can keep lifting up and helping resource partners, pushing back against the status quo, and inviting people to see a new way of doing things, then she'll keep going. And with each step she never stops asking: Is this truly reflective of the types of equitable partnerships that we want to build? Who benefits? Could there be a better way?

She may have been born into an old story, but Patty is determined to write a new story, and she is doing it by embracing *The Weaver's Way*, and leveraging her privileges to create change.

LEVERAGING PRIVILEGE

Because you're reading this book, I know we share at least two of the same privileges: literacy, and the ability to understand the most widely spoken language in the world. These may seem inconsequential, but after so many years living and working with people for whom this is not the case, I've come to more deeply appreciate the advantages they provide. Take Loida, whom you've already met.

Loida, like many other indigenous Guatemalan women of her age, never went to school and is unable to read and write. She speaks limited Spanish, preferring to speak in her native T'zutujil, one of the twenty-four national languages spoken in the country. If she had gone to school, however, she would have been subjected to *castilianization,* a government policy designed to assimilate and acculturate Mayan children. Castilianization permitted only minimal use of indigenous languages and then only to further Spanish fluency.

Neither of Loida's options seem very appealing to me, as someone who had access to free public education in my mother tongue. But I never fully appreciated what a *privilege* it was and how I could use that privilege to shape change until I came to see the world through Loida's eyes.

We all have privileges. Some undoubtedly more than others. The privileges I'm talking about are the advantages or preferential treatment from which we benefit that are related to what I call "the birth lottery." Factors such as our place of origin, our citizenship status, our parents, our education, our ability, our gender identity, our place in a hierarchy. Or whether or not we are educated in our preferred language. But when it comes to *The Weaver's Way* framework, I believe the more constructive discussion is not *who* has it but *how* we use it.

One of the blessings that comes from building bridging relationships—relationships that respect our differences while also celebrating our commonalities—is that it allows people to discover their privileges. My relationship with Abigail and Loida helped me become more adept at seeing privileges that I'd previously overlooked or simply taken for granted.

In a similar way, seeing themselves through my eyes has helped both Abigail and Loida to better recognize the gifts they bring. Mutual recognition of unique value.

There is another hidden surprise. When society is made up of many bonded tribal groups, privilege is a blunt instrument used as a form of control of one group over another. In bridging relationships however, privilege is much more nuanced. Rather than a weapon, it becomes a tool we can leverage in order to shape change in service to our relationships. In service to the greater good.

KNOW THYSELF

All we've discussed so far in the Weaver's Journey of Becoming is part of a process of developing self-knowledge. *Know thyself* is a command that's been repeated hundreds of times in many different faiths and philosophies as far back as Aristotle yet remains just as relevant today to the work of shaping change.

Why?

Because it is through the process of developing self-knowledge that we learn to develop a compassionate heart, curious mind, and courageous spirit. It's something that I call *wholeheartedness*. And it's essential to the work of being a Weaver.

Through wholeheartedness we become more curious about who we are and how our mind works. We learn to bear witness with compassion and empathy. We are able to approach difficult situations with greater tenderness and acceptance, without becoming overwhelmed, bitter, or twisted. We learn to master our defense system so that instead of being a liability, it becomes a tool for living with precarity and navigating the uncharted waters of change. We learn to be productive in vulnerability and trust ourselves. And we discover the magical alchemy of emotions, transmuting our anger, fear, grief, and despair into powerful forces for change.

This inner work—the practice of wholeheartedness—is necessary to cultivate the proactive courage and creative consciousness required to shape change. But let me emphasize the word *practice*. This is a journey of becoming, not being. A continuous journey, not a destination. It's a lifelong practice that offers continuous opportunities for growth, learning, and insight.

Some of the exercises and reflections in this book may help you with your practice. But there's so much more to discover. There may be times when you choose to walk your path alone, using books or other resources to help you. I've included a handful of suggestions that I've found useful in the More Information section in Part III of this book. At other times, you might find it useful to join a community of practice, a group of people who can help you deepen your learning and discovery. Many Weavers I know have their own religious faiths or spiritual traditions that they're part of. And at other times, you may find that a coach, mentor, or other professional who can accompany you for some of your journey becomes helpful. I've done all three at different times in my own journey. Most importantly, do what's right for you. It's your journey.

SUMMARY

- Learning to shape change that is meaningful and transformative means committing to an inner journey of truth and transparency that takes courage, bravery, and sacrifice.
- This journey invites us to pay attention and see the world as it really is and train ourselves to bear witness to pain and suffering while maintaining a compassionate heart, curious mind, and courageous spirit.
- We can be supported on this journey by building connections that cross traditional divides such as race, religion, class, gender, and geography. These kinds of relationships help you to identify your privileges, then leverage them for creating change.

EXERCISES

1. The continuum of the human story.
Take a moment to reflect on the continuum of the human story. Now situate yourself on this through line. Are there elements of this story that make you uncomfortable? Are there truths you're avoiding? What might happen if you turned to face that which you have been avoiding? How might you begin to get comfortable with that discomfort?

2. Invest in social capital—for yourself and others.
They say that the quality of your life is determined by the quality of your relationships. Look around you. What kinds of relationships do you have in your life? Are they monochromatic or kaleidoscopic? Are they bonding relationships or bridging relationships?

Social capital is essential for resilience. Strong capital is built through a diversity of investments. Look around your community and place of work. Where/with whom might you be able to start building more bridging networks?

3. Practice wholeheartedness.
Wholeheartedness is the ability to work with a compassionate heart, curious mind, and courageous spirit. One of Patty's practices is to always let herself be guided by the community leaders that she is working to serve.

What kinds of practices or activities are you currently engaged in that help you work toward wholeheartedness? How might your work change today if you could bring a little more wholeheartedness? What one practice might you try today to help cultivate that?

CHAPTER 8

WEAVING FOR CHANGE

 When patterns are broken, new worlds emerge.

— TULI KUPFERBERG

It is a Saturday in 2016, market day, far up in the remote highlands of Guatemala in an area that's predominantly Quiché Maya. I stand surrounded by a cacophony of noise and color, jostled in every direction by women with baskets full of produce, men carrying herculean loads strapped across their foreheads, and small children with sticky hands and bright red mouths.

Next to me is Abigail, and in front of us, blending into the riotous overflow of brightly colored textiles, is a young woman. Her arms are full of yet more offerings, and her smile is full of hope for a successful sale. Standing still in a place like this always feels to me like standing on the edge of the ocean and trying to stop the tide rushing in. My instinct is to just let go and let myself be carried along on the surge of bodies, but I resist. We are on a mission.

I look down at the garment in my hands—a second-hand güipil (Mayan blouse)—studying first the geometric designs on the front then flipping it over to examine the reverse. I glance across at Abigail, raising my eyebrows in silent inquiry, and she gives me a small shake of her head. Nope.

I look out across the heads of the crowd. There are not many places in the world where my height places me in the top percentile of people, and while I feel uncomfortably conspicuous, I'm grateful right now for the view. "That's it," I tell Abigail as I scan the market stalls in both directions. "We've checked them all."

Under Abigail's guidance, I've been searching the market for a handmade güipil from this region that I can take home as a gift for my mother, whose passion is costume and textiles. But we've had no luck. We are disappointed, but not surprised. Mass-produced güipiles are emerging in marketplaces throughout the region. Nowadays it's all too easy to find yourself in a community market—even one like this more than a day's drive from the nearest large city—and discover almost everything is machine made.

THE INDUSTRIALIZATION OF CHANGE

According to Amanda Denham, who has researched the effects of shifting political economies on the dress of Maya people, a lot has changed since the country opened up to the outside world and Western tourists (and ideologies) came flooding in. Prior to the 1970s, the production of textiles was much more a function of cultural values and social relationships than finance, often gifted and traded between community members. "Güipiles were not goods that were efficiently produced and sold at their highest price," writes Denham. "(However) the economic rupture of global capitalism and tourism impacted the production, consumption, and exchange of güipiles from a localized object to a wholly commodified product."[1]

It is now as common to see a young Maya woman wearing a used T-shirt sporting one of the ubiquitous global Western brands like Abercrombie or Coca-Cola imported by the ton from American thrift stores and sold on trestle tables piled high with the discards of the capitalist dream as it is to see her wearing her traditional dress.

The industrialization of weaving. Progress, it is called. But at what cost? Is the loss of art, culture, tradition, and connection—elements known to strengthen the social fabric and bring communities together —an acceptable price to pay? Or might there be more serious consequences from allowing them to become just another forgotten footnote in the pervasive old story and its harmful patterns? And, perhaps most importantly, who gets to decide?

I share this story because I believe our change processes have been subjected to the same influences. Much of the impetus behind writing this book came from years of frustration at seeing firsthand the impact of unsuccessful aid projects. Working with communities tired of being the recipients of well-intentioned "fixes" ultimately doomed to fail, or being the unwitting objects of a project designed to be the crowning glory in someone else's CV.

I cringe every time I hear the BBC feature another innovative, technological solution dreamed up by students and academics at elite educational institutions, trying to solve the problems of poor brown people on the other side of the world.

Just like weaving, our approach to change has been industrialized, just another machine to perpetuate the oppressive paradigms of the old story. Take a look around at different examples of change processes unfolding. Whether it's in your workplace, kids' school, or your local community. Can you see the now familiar patterns of the old tropes? Top-down models, externally imposed solutions, decision making and resources controlled by powerful Leaders, and command-and-control thinking that assumes change is a linear process.

We need to move past our industrialized, Western-centric approach if we want to contribute toward creating meaningful and transformative change. And to do that, we need to take a closer look at the process of how change is created.

THE WEAVING LORES

When it comes to shaping meaningful and transformative change, it's not a question of "by any means possible." In Part I, when we examined the role that stories and narratives play in shaping change, we talked about how solutions that don't question assumptions reinforce the dominant patterns. We also discussed the idea that those patterns may hold certain values and beliefs that are not aligned with the kind of society we wish to be a part of. This is why, as Weavers, it is so vital to mindfully focus our attention on *how* we choose to shape change.

The Weaver's Way Framework

The Weaver — Weaving

In doing research for this book, I looked back at all that had happened since we started SERES, looking at changes I believed were successful and changes I felt had been unsuccessful. I also looked at case studies from other countries including Myanmar, Malaysia, Thailand, Botswana, Vietnam, and Switzerland (many of these case studies are connected to the work of the people whose stories are included in The Weaver's Guild). My goal in doing so was to see if I could identify commonalities across these different projects that would help answer the question about *how* we shape meaningful and transformative change.

Out of the stories and experiences, three patterns emerged. Firstly, regardless of geography and demographics, all the case studies I looked at put the people who were closest to the problem at the center of the change process. Secondly, they were clear that their goal was long-term change processes rather than time-bound, project-based interventions. And finally, there was a clear connection between the solution and the specificity of the place in which the solution was implemented.

In this next section, we'll explore in more detail each of these three patterns, which I have called Weaving Lores. But before we do, it's worth taking a moment to qualify what successful change is, since my idea of successful change may not be the same as yours. So for the purposes of *The Weaver's Way*, the change processes that were deemed successful were:

- Regenerative—they put more in than they took out
- Valued and built different forms of capital, such as social and knowledge capital
- Allowed for *dignified* participation of all people(s), especially those most impacted by the change
- Were locally led and locally owned
- Created long-term benefits beyond the specific activities that took place

With that shared understanding, let's take a closer look at the three Weaving Lores.

LORE 1: PEOPLE-DRIVEN PARTNERSHIPS

In SERES's second year, Antonio and I set ourselves what was for us at the time a very ambitious goal: to host a five-day, cross-border (Guatemala and El Salvador) sustainability summit, bringing together different youth groups we'd been working with over the last eighteen months. We had a list of one hundred names and what felt like an even longer list of hurdles to overcome. Border crossing permissions for underage participants, finding the funds not just for the event but for transport to and from the communities for youth who were unable to pay, convincing parents to let their children—particularly the young women—to be away from home. It seemed that every time we solved one obstacle two more came up.

I'd been staying the week in El Salvador where we planned to host the summit, going with Antonio to visit communities during the day and coming back to sleep at his family's home in El Papaturro in the evenings. El Papaturro lies about three kilometers off the main highway down a bumpy dirt road, and Antonio's home is one of the first, right where the road branches to form the community's two main streets (four-wheel-drive-only dirt tracks).

Every day that we went out, Antonio always planned to ensure we were home by early afternoon.

"What do you have to do?" I would quiz him, thinking of all the farm chores that I was familiar with from my own childhood.

"Nothing, just hang out," he would shrug.

And sure enough, every day on arriving home he proceeded to do just that, leaning back against the concrete block wall that surrounded his house, a faded yellow hand towel draped over his shoulder to wipe sweat and flick away the occasional fly.

"Are you waiting for someone?" I asked, curious.

"No" came the short reply. But there he would sit for at least an hour, calling out to people as they went by. Some would stop to chat, while other conversations took place as a quick exchange of shouted words that faded down the road.

Driving back home that Friday afternoon I was hot, tired, and more than a little frustrated. I'd been noticing, more and more, Antonio's habit of active loitering. It seemed that no matter how much we had to do, wherever we went he would get waylaid in conversation or distracted by an invitation into someone's home for coffee or lunch. And then we had to come home early so he could hang out.

As Antonio opened the gate in the chain-link fence and I maneuvered the car up into the small concrete driveway, I thought grumpily about how I needed to teach Antonio about the merits of a polite refusal. I parked in silence, and we headed off to our usual afternoon positions: Antonio out in front of the house, me with my laptop up in the fork of a scrawny, bare-limbed tree I shared with an equally scrawny chicken. It was one of the few places I could catch a patchy internet signal. Still feeling peevish, I took a deep sigh, trying to block out the conversations drifting in from the road and turned my attention back to my desperate attempts to get a successful Google hit for "minibus hire El Salvador."

After another unsuccessful Googling session, I sat down later that evening with Antonio to go over the list of things we still had to work out. Catering, logistics, and transport—I'd come up blank on all of them. But as I read out each item, like a magician conjuring out of thin air, Antonio produced names and numbers. It generally went something like this: "The twins' mother's cousin said they would donate two bags of corn that will make enough for 150 tortillas," or "Don Oscar did a job last year for a man that has two minibuses, and says he'll get us one of those."

"Who's Don Oscar?" I asked.

"The man with the cow that's lame because Doña Frida's dog, Lobo, got out last Saturday when Rafael came home drunk from a dance and bit the cow," he replied matter-of-factly, as though this would mean something to me.

I bit my lip to stop myself asking if it was Lobo or Rafael who bit the cow and just stared at him, baffled. Then all of a sudden a light bulb went off in my head. I smiled and then, unable to help myself, started laughing. I finally understood. Antonio hadn't been fruitlessly wasting time. He'd been networking. Just doing so in a way that I'd never been taught to appreciate.

In my early professional career, I'd been taught that networking was a verb. Something you did at events and conferences where people walked around making superficial small talk while trying to determine whether or not the person they were talking to (me) was worth their time. It had always felt like a highly transactional process fraught with unchecked power dynamics. *Quid pro quo* is the phrase that comes to mind. My memories of it were that it was generally unpleasant—unless there was alcohol involved. Then I would drink too much cheap wine and push the discomfort to the next day when I would nurse my headache and reflect that it'd likely all been for nothing anyway.

But I'm certain that for Antonio this idea of networking was as alien to him as I was to the chicken with whom I now regularly shared a perch. For him (Antonio, not the chicken) networking wasn't a verb but an outcome. The result of strong, authentic relationships built over time. With his house so conveniently located at the only entrance into the community, in those moments that Antonio dedicated to "hanging out" he would greet and talk to almost everyone. Kids coming home from school, farmers returning from the fields, people visiting relatives, and folks coming home from work. With a simple exchange or easy question, he not only got the news and current affairs, but he invested into his network. Antonio knew these people understood what was needed and how to get things done, and he also knew that those relationships were vital to the work we wanted to do.

Looking back with an even deeper respect for Antonio and no small amount of embarrassment on my part, I realize now that Antonio instinctively understood in a way I had yet to fully appreciate, the first Weaving Lore. People-Driven Partnerships.

Someone else who understands this, and who has applied it to those nightmarish events (conferences) I described earlier is Topher Wilkins.

WEAVER: TOPHER WILKINS

Featuring a conference convener in the Weaver's Guild may seem like a strange choice, but I wanted to bring it in because of how much attention social networks are receiving in today's modern economy. Adam Grant argues in his book *Power Moves* that networks are the new form of power.[2] Respectable business schools teach their students about the importance of strong ties and weak ties in network structures, and social media is one of the fastest growing industries in the tech sector. And while it's heartening to see that the importance of relationships and the acknowledgement of our interdependence is making a mainstream appearance, it seems that this, too, has not escaped our old patterns.

I meet new people in a business setting and explain to them that I'm a Weaver, and they nod knowingly. Then invariably a few months later I'll receive a note from them offering to pay me if I could just introduce them to so-and-so. I happily connect good people doing good work with other good people doing good work. I don't sell relationships.

With a recent occurrence fresh in my mind, I reflect on this with Topher as we wait for our Zoom meeting to start. With his line of work, I'm sure this must happen to him a lot more than me. "Oh yeah," he agreed. "But the good thing, I guess, is that it's an easy way to identify someone who just doesn't get it."

What's there to "get," you might ask, about connecting and convening people? Plenty, it turns out. Topher describes himself as an "impact convener," which means he brings people together with the goal of creating social good. Remember that Funders and Founders event from Chapter 1? Well, it's that kind of thing. Only very, very different.

As Topher explained, many of his peers in the convening space use what he describes as "a very industrialized, patriarchal way of bringing people together. Plenaries, keynotes, 'experts' on the stage, sponsored logos splashed around everywhere." The problem is that this way of bringing people together goes *against* the work of creating meaningful change. "It's disconcerting," he explained to me, "continuing to bring people together in that way is actually making the problems worse. Those kinds of events stratify an already disjointed community. They bolster egos and reinforce unhealthy power dynamics. We get division where we need unity."

The alternative to this format is what has come to be known as the *unconference* model, an approach Topher wholeheartedly embraces through his role as CEO of Opportunity Collaboration. Every year, the organization brings together people from around the world who are working to tackle issues of injustice, attracting leaders from across the spectrum and bringing them together for a four-day retreat—at Club Med!

The irony of coming together to solve global poverty at an all-expenses paid resort in Mexico is not lost on Topher, but with the skills of the integrative thinker on full display, it's a tension Topher and the rest of the OC team are willing to live with. The people who started Opportunity Collaboration, or OC as it's more commonly known, put a lot of intention and thought into designing the conference.

Their aim was to create a space for real, authentic dialogue and conversation in a way that helped equalize some of the power imbalances that often occurred within the changemaking ecosystem. And what better way than at the beach with friends and family?

While I was skeptical at first, I have to admit that after a few years being involved in OC as both a participant and a moderator, they've done a pretty good job.

The OC approach is based on an understanding that meaningful and transformative change happens best when we get a chance to come together as our whole selves, not buttoned up in a suit, masks on hand ready to make a pitch. It seeks to give people an opportunity to laugh together, play together, and have myriad different shared experiences that help build authentic, meaningful relationships.

This is another place where Topher sees his role differently. A typical convener's goal is to be helping "get deals done." ABC it's called in the business world. Always be closing. This is the opposite—an opening or unfolding of possibility. Topher sees himself in service of fostering relationships rather than transactions. "I work under the notion that if we can get a broad representation of changemakers together and facilitate the time and space for relationships that are built on trust, then long term they will work more effectively together to create meaningful change."

One of the aspects that I suspect makes Topher so effective in what he does is his willingness to model what he asks participants to do. In between showing up as the host, the curator, the convener, and the director, Topher is there as a dad—his three boys are never far away—and a husband as he works side by side with Jorian, "the love of his life." "The key to being effective," said Topher, "is allowing yourself to be as personal and vulnerable as you can be."

I THINK ABOUT TOPHER AS I FIRST MET HIM, WITH HIS SUNHAT, SHORTS, AND flip flops, three small blond boys tugging him in various directions while he warmly greeted the arriving conference delegates. He's not that different from Antonio sitting shirtless with a hand towel draped over one shoulder, shouting greetings and making small talk with people as they make their way home after a long day. They both understand almost instinctively that the keys to shaping change are relationships built on trust, not transactions. Bridges, not bonds.

As humans, we exist in a vibrating web of interdependence. Connected by delicate gossamer threads of relationships that are constantly changing, dissolving, and emerging. To recognize the existence of this web is to acknowledge the importance of respecting the experience of all people, at all times. And understanding that dignity, both individual and collective, is connected to our ability to participate fully in the structures of society.

As we have discussed and seen in examples, a hallmark of the old narrative for creating change is externally driven solutions that are imposed onto certain groups or communities, often with little room for their input. The sad irony being those closest to the problems often have important insights as well as untapped resources, which are invaluable for creating transformative solutions.

People-driven partnerships are the opposite. In many ways, this first Lore is really just an extension of the Laws of Interconnectedness that we explored in Chapter 6. So let's look at what this first Lore means for the work of shaping change.

First, we must be willing to engage with others as part of finding solutions. Too many times community consultation takes place after a project has already been designed and budgeted. This makes the process of listening and engaging tokenistic. Honoring people-driven partnerships requires listening intently and respectfully, ensuring opportunities exist for all voices to be included in dialogue and decision-making and being guided by what those closest to the change deem as important and valuable.

Second, it means finding ways to facilitate collaborative and cooperative approaches. These approaches need to understand and embrace diversity across cultures, social groups, communities, and individuals. They need to understand and value the diverse experiences, resources, perspectives, and preferences that exist. And they need to acknowledge and value other knowledge systems and expertise apart from the traditional "expert," such as indigenous wisdom and contextual or lived experience.

Last but not least, it means recognizing that consequential decisions should be made by those who must live with the consequences and seeing everyone involved as partners rather than passive recipients. Prioritizing the kinds of caring and connection that nurture these partnerships. Thinking about measures of success defined in the collective not the individual and not putting profits, programs, or products ahead of people or the planet.

In SERES we did this in many different ways, such as providing participatory processes wherein youth were able to provide both input and feedback to our strategic planning and having youth alumni elect representatives to the board of directors. Topher does it by creating gathering spaces where *all* voices have the opportunity to be heard and people have the chance to show up as their full selves. Patty does it in her advocacy to put local leaders and locally led organizations at the center of the development process.

I've seen it used in other situations: parent/teacher committees at schools that hold workshops to listen and discover how students feel about a particular issue. A scholarship program wherein the scholarship recipients are able to determine the kind of support they need. And an indigenous entrepreneurship training program built on the values and beliefs of the Maya cosmovision not Western ideology.

How do we know when we're doing this successfully? It's a question I posed to Topher.

Topher's experience, which echoes my own, is that when you begin working in this way you discover a richness to life that has nothing to do with financial capital. "I would like to think the future that we're creating is one where success is not defined by the white picket fence and two-car garage but is far more hinged to our relationships with one another. On our ability to connect deeply, to find that common ground and bravely explore differences, realizing our fates are bound together. That's the legacy I want to be part of."

The future we're creating. Not a place we're heading but a world that we are calling forth. It's a legacy that I, too, want to be part of.

LORE 2: PROCESS-CENTRIC APPROACHES

Back in my consulting engineering days, I did a lot of project management on large and complex projects. Project management uses a certain type of thinking that sees the world as linear and predictable. It assumes certain inputs will trigger certain outputs within predetermined timeframes, which then lead to certain results. And anything interrupting that logic is a problem that must be solved. I call this a *project-centric* approach.

When I began my quest to understand how to create meaningful and transformative change, I was surprised to see this project-centric approach was widespread. In fact, it seemed to be the modus operandi for almost any change process. But while command-and-control thinking and deficit-based problem solving may work in certain environments, out in the wider world of creating societal change, it is far less successful.

A project-centric approach works well in situations that are orderly, predictable, and controllable. Serving one hundred meals each day at the soup kitchen, for example. The problem is that transformative change is not so regular and mechanical. Transformative change works on both people and systems, creating the conditions that can cause the change itself to be self-sustaining. To stick with our soup kitchen example, a kind of transformative change would be finding a way to ensure that over time fewer people need the services of the soup kitchen itself. In that scenario you would likely find a project-centric approach wouldn't work. That's because both people and systems are unpredictable and ever-changing, which means linear, project-centric thinking doesn't work.

This may all seem like common sense, but I can assure you it is far from commonplace in the formal change sector. I remember during my early days with SERES being introduced to a tool commonly referred to as the logical framework, log frame or LGA. We would never get funding, I was told, without this. Every project, every application, required us to meticulously detail how each input would have a given output, which would then contribute to carefully defined outcomes, and finally, impact.

Perhaps now after the entire world has gone through two years of a global pandemic, we can appreciate how illogical this logical framework is when it comes to shaping change. Causes and effects, it turns out, don't necessarily flow in a predictable way. "I don't think even God could fill one of these in!" I would mutter to Antonio as we tried to fit our round peg into a square hole.

It was during one of these sessions, feeling exasperated, that I started to do a little digging about where this tool had come from. And I was somewhat stunned to discover it traced its origins back to the Pentagon, where it was used as a planning approach for the US military. Do we really believe we can create transformative change—change that contributes toward more peaceful and just societies—with this as our building block? I added this to my list of Old Stories and Patterns and set about looking for examples and approaches that were part of a new way of shaping change. I called these process-centric approaches.

It was this ongoing search for process-centric approaches that first drew me to the work of Joyce Yee, one of the Weavers from The Weaver's Guild whom you met earlier. For the last six years, Joyce has conducted extensive research to better understand the principles and practices behind successful change processes throughout Southeast Asia, and her conclusions are startlingly similar to my own.

"The traditional approach," said Joyce, "is focused on neat problem solving, time-based and bounded." It's the perfect setup to allow heroes to parachute in and save the day but not for creating transformational change. "The evidence shows that coming in and out like that just doesn't work," argued Yee. So what does?

From the different examples I've come across over the years, process-centric approaches have two things in common.

Firstly, process-centric approaches recognize that our lives, our communities are always in process. This is what is known as a living systems perspective. Nothing in our world exists in isolation. It is always in connection to other people and other systems in a dynamic process of adaptation, evolution and emergence. Remember principle four talks about the importance of agility. To shape transformative change we must learn to be flexible, responsive, and reflexive, rather than trying to control every outcome to a predetermined set of goals.

Secondly, as Joyce put in, "They must realize they're part of the fabric they are weaving...part of the threads that hold that community together." Our metaphor of the backstrap loom illustrates this perfectly. One of the distinctive characteristics of this particular loom is that the weaver's own body becomes an integral part of the tool. As Loida prepares to weave, she first binds herself into the loom and in doing so, becomes an extension of the loom itself.

In a similar way, a Weaver must also embed themselves into the process. As Joyce explained, "The job is to build infrastructure...to build systems, processes, capacity, relationships...In this way, you may weave in and out, but you never extract yourself."

Thus, a process-centric approach is not about applying a one-size-fits-all formula but about being *in* process as change happens. Donella Meadows, our leading systems thinker, summarizes it perfectly: "Living successfully in a world of systems requires more of us than our ability to calculate. It requires our full humanity."[3]

LORE 3: ROOTED IN PLACE

The impacts of industrialized textile production on Guatemala's indigenous communities encompasses much more than a consideration of economics and the availability of cheap clothing. In Guatemala, as in many cultures that still use weaving, weavers have an important role to play not just in strengthening the social fabric of the community, but in maintaining a vital connection to place. The different colors and patterns are not only aesthetic but often deeply symbolic. A weaving can thus be seen as a collection of stories about people and place, revealing not only the area of origin and the kinship of the wearer but oftentimes other mathematical, astronomical, and natural truths.

A weaver like Loida helps to preserve invaluable cultural heritage —a connection to the past and reminder of an ancient civilization. And she also helps to preserve a connection to the future, one that embraces diversity. A quiet resistance against forces that would automate and homogenize everything in the name of progress and efficiency.

In the same way, a Weaver's individual efforts can be seen as part of a greater effort that's both longitudinal and collective. An intergenerational through line, if you will, that's grounded in place and connected to culture. It's what Joyce Yee talks about in her research as a *culturally led* approach. "It's important to respect existing knowledge and practices," said Joyce. "Grounding in place, culture, and locality is key."

Connection to place is important not only for the knowledge and wisdom it can generate, but because it's an essential component of building an inclusive and thriving future. Think about the paradigms from the old narrative. One of the trademarks of colonization was to disconnect, often violently, people from place. While an economic system built on extractivism allowed consequences such as pollution and contamination to be labeled as no more than "externalities."

With what effect? In those early travels through Mexico and Guatemala, I saw in vivid detail just how closely interlinked environmental degradation and economic poverty were. Where one existed, the other was never far away. Connection to healthy, vibrant places is what fosters and sustains communities and enables them to thrive. Without it, there can be no justice and equality, and no transformative change.

Someone who has a deep respect for connection to place and valuing the indigenous wisdom and knowledge that come with it is Professor Richie Moalosi, a professor in the Department of Industrial

Design and Technology at the University of Botswana. He is an advocate for the decolonization and indigenization of education and curriculum development and agrees strongly with the idea that processes and practices that aren't based on local knowledge cannot be sustainable. His work, as you will see, also demonstrates how the three Weaving Lores are used together to create meaningful and transformative change.

During my time with SERES, International Service Learning projects saw a rise in popularity in the United States, and Guatemala became a popular destination for student trips. For those not familiar with the concept, service learning is an educational approach wherein a student complements their theoretical work by volunteering with an organization (usually a non-profit or social service group) to deepen their understanding of what is being taught.

But I didn't like the taste of the Kool-Aid. While I acknowledged service learning could be a considerable formative experience for the students, I just couldn't shake the sense that it was both cruel and insensitive to frame learning around someone else's condition and dangerously misleading to let young people believe that in two weeks they could somehow create any significant change.

Every time I was propositioned with a new service-learning project, I would hear Dr. Lilla Watson's words echoing in my head: "If you've come to help me, you're wasting your time." After a few early attempts, it was clear the service-learning model did not align with SERES's ethos, and so despite subsequent invitations, we largely declined to participate. And years of watching these projects play out in different communities across Guatemala had only served to fortify my skepticism.

In January 2020, sitting in my small apartment in Turin, Italy, I was flicking through the weekly syllabus for the master's program I was studying in and reading about the upcoming module on service learning as a tool for social innovation." I took a deep breath, rolled my eyes, and prepared for battle. I'm happy to admit, however, that not only did I lose that battle, but I was completely disarmed from the get-go.

The moment I walked into the classroom to see an African standing up front, my resistance slipped away. Professor Moalosi's presence was a welcome change to a program that in my opinion had been entirely too dominated by a traditional Western viewpoint on creating change. I felt grateful for the simple fact of being exposed to a greater diversity of thought and opinion and readied myself to put away my judgements and listen.

But it turns out, I had even more to be grateful to him for. Because Professor Moalosi helped me to reevaluate my ideas about service learning, opening my eyes to a wonderful approach that incorporates the three Weaving Lores to create a more collaborative and mutually beneficial experience for student-community engagement.

WEAVER: RICHIE MOALOSI

Moalosi's work and research focuses largely on communities in rural Botswana where he uses an approach that he describes as the integration of the philosophy of Ubuntu in the cocreation of community projects. "Communities are tired of being someone else's research or learning subject," said Moalosi. "Ubuntu is our lens, it comes from our culture. It teaches us about values such as generosity, respect, forgiveness, community spirit, cooperation, togetherness, sharing, reconciliation, trust, empathy, collaboration, interdependence, spirituality, collective responsibilities, harmony, love, consensus building, and interpersonal relationships among people. Co-creation is an act of collective creativity. We bring these two concepts together to transform people into active partners for the creation of future value."

What this looks like in practice is a people-driven, process-centric, and place-based approach that creates opportunities for students and specialists to support a community's own internally driven change processes.

I asked Professor Moalosi to tell me a little more about his work.

"To start with," he begins, "I put people at the heart of everything. I believe that whoever they are, they have the ability to determine their own development." He described his role as a guide, facilitator, and catalyst. "I'm here to solve with, not for, and the number one thing required to do this is to never undermine someone's belief in themselves. My role is to convince them that whatever they want to do, it is achievable."

Focusing on people in this way is important for two other reasons. It fosters ownership, and it unlocks indigenous knowledge, both of which are required for meaningful and transformative change. As Professor Moalosi explained, indigenous knowledge does not have to be indigenous in the traditional definition. It's about recognizing that there exists a dynamic, ever-changing body of knowledge and skills that a community accumulates over time as it adapts to local culture and the environment.

And a Weaver's work is to tap into that. "We start with what people know, the way they do things, how and what they see. Then we look for the connection between 'this is what we have been doing' and 'this is where we are going,' and build on that," he explained.

There is no doubt that this approach takes more time than the typical (Western) service learning or voluntourism project, but Moalosi has no problem with that. "That's what it takes," he said simply. He told about one community they've been working with for some time with the Basarwa or San people, more commonly known as the Kalahari Bushmen. Moalosi's willingness to invest time, to be in process is particularly important for the Basarwa people. Their culture, of particular fascination by Western anthropologists, makes them one of the most well-documented indigenous cultures in the world.

It has also, as one researcher put it, "robbed them of the ability to tell their own stories." "We have been told many times by the village elders," said Moalosi, "so many people have come here to research, but we never see anything as a result. They leave, and we are still here." It is a continuation of the extractive mindset that we discussed in Chapter 1, and an all-too-common occurrence when the research subjects or beneficiaries are representatives of marginalized or disenfranchised communities.

To build trust and prove themselves as trustworthy, the first thing they did was to stay with the community for two weeks. "There was no agenda," said Moalosi, "but to be there." This is timefullness in practice. They sat around the campfire, danced, and told stories. "You have to be curious, show you are willing to invest time listening and learning. Immerse yourself in the process of discovery. Relationships are more important than milestones. This is about building trust and connection, building the social infrastructure required to co-create something meaningful." Moalosi knew that if they tried to rush the process with an externally driven sense of urgency, they would undermine the trust and never gain the approval of the village elders.

Toward the end of the two weeks, there was an important shift among the visitors and the community members. People went from asking "What can you do for us/what can we do for you?" to asking "What can we do together?" "From there," said Moalosi, "it was easy."

Local innovators, with the support of an outside team of specialists, have designed and built a number of different prototypes to help address local community needs, including improving the method of processing morama beans (*Tylosema esculentum*), a local leguminous oilseed native to the Kalahari Desert; a foot-powered washing machine; and a wheelchair designed for sandy desert conditions.

The community also led the establishment of an innovation center, a free-to-access communal space that can be used for the ongoing design and development of new low-tech innovations.

As Joyce Yee's research demonstrates, "When change is nonindigenous —top-down, driven from outside, not responsive to the needs of the community—it just doesn't have any huge, lasting effect."

Using the Weaving Lores to shape change offers an important reframe: from passivity and powerlessness to activity and opportunity; from the top-down, problem-focused narrative of old to a bottom-up, asset-based solution that helps communities build local assets and strengthen local ownership, as demonstrated through Moalosi's work.

But perhaps most importantly, as Moalosi points out, is that through this approach the community had the opportunity to tell a new story. A story in which they became the custodians of their own empowerment. In doing so, they dispelled the doubts about their capabilities and ingenuity created by the many years of discrimination and social injustice.

People, process, place has become a non-negotiable mantra that guides all of my work, and it has never failed me. I can quickly and easily recognize people and organizations that value this way of working, and those that don't. But as different as it is from what we have been taught about how change is done, I know that it can be challenging at first to understand how these Weaving Lores work in practice. So let me illustrate with a story about a group of people and a place which will forever hold a tender and precious place in my heart.

SUMMARY

- Shaping change is not a question of "by any means possible." How we do it is as important as what we do.
- The three Weaving Lores help to guide how we shape change by grounding our work in people-driven partnerships, process-centric approaches, and place-based solutions.
- The Weaver Lores should be used as part of an emergent strategy—one that is constantly evolving and responding to changes in the ecosystem, just like a living system.

EXERCISES

1. PEOPLE, PROCESS, PLACE: HOW ARE YOU USING THEM?
Take a moment to reflect on places where you're working to shape change, whether it's in your community, business, or even family.

2. WHOSE VOICES OR EXPERIENCES ARE MOST INVOLVED IN SHAPING SOLUTIONS AND DECIDING OUTCOMES?
Who are you not listening to, want to listen to more deeply, or want to get to know better? How flexible and adaptable are you in your approach? Do existing knowledge and practices inform what you do and how you do it?

If you'd like to incorporate more of the Weaving Lores, try by asking: Who is here? What is the voice of this place, these people? What are the stories asking to be told? Then listen deeply for the answers and let them guide the process.

CHAPTER 9
FINCA ULEW: PLACE OF FIRE

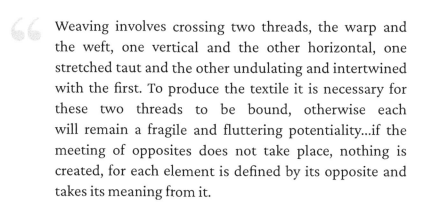

Weaving involves crossing two threads, the warp and the weft, one vertical and the other horizontal, one stretched taut and the other undulating and intertwined with the first. To produce the textile it is necessary for these two threads to be bound, otherwise each will remain a fragile and fluttering potentiality...if the meeting of opposites does not take place, nothing is created, for each element is defined by its opposite and takes its meaning from it.

— DARIO VACARENGI, *KILIM HISTORY AND SYMBOLS*, AS QUOTED IN *THE ART OF WEAVING A LIFE* BY SUSAN BARRETT MERRILL

A few years into SERES's existence, an idea began to emerge from across the youth network—to give SERES a home. Over and over, the idea kept surfacing. A safe space. A gathering place. Somewhere for young people to come together, share ideas, and learn the skills they would need to build stronger, more resilient communities in an increasingly climate-uncertain future.

I was excited by the possibilities, but also somewhat overwhelmed at the prospect. How could we make this happen? Where would we get the resources? Was this the best way to serve our youth? I had many questions, and very few answers. But even as I sat in that place of uncertainty, one thing was crystal clear. We couldn't repeat the same mistakes we'd made previously. This wasn't going to be a business-as-usual development project. If we were going to make this work, then we had to follow The Weaver's Way.

And so we began with almost three years talking with youth from across our network, listening deeply, paying attention to what was emerging, building our collective dream. As we did, the idea began to take shape: a living-learning campus to support a new generation of young leaders to develop the skills and tools they would need to help their communities transform from surviving to thriving.

NO MORE WALLS

As the vision became clearer, we started to ask: where was the place that would make this possible? We searched for over eighteen months until we finally found it. A twenty-five-acre farm, or *finca*, located about forty minutes from our main office in Antigua. Perched on the Pacific side of the volcanic chain that runs through the country, right where the land drops away to the fertile coastal plains.

It's an area of Guatemala that's (still) reminiscent of feudal society. The landscape is dominated by large sugarcane and banana plantations, whose wealthy owners live mostly in the capital city. Interspersed with crime-ridden urban slums and shanty towns whose inhabitants work on the plantations at a rate of around one US dollar per ton of cut cane. The power divide and distrust between rich landlords and peasant farmers here runs wide and deep, announced loudly and clearly by the towering walls topped with broken glass and razor wire that surround the fincas, overseen by 24/7 security guards armed with pistols and shotguns.

Our new land didn't have walls, but it did have a resident caretaker. A man about my own age, short and solidly built, named Marco Antonio. Marco Antonio had grown up nearby on a finca purchased by a group of peasant farmers, including Marco Antonio's parents, under a land reform program designed for the resettlement of refugees who fled during the civil conflict. Land rich but dirt poor, as the saying goes, Marco Antonio never had the opportunity to go to school or learn to read and write. His job as caretaker six out of seven days was to keep the grass down (using nothing but a machete) and discouraging people from nearby communities from chopping down trees to use for firewood.

When we purchased the property, we knew which side of the power divide we would be placed on, and the advice from those on that side poured in:

"Fire your caretaker. If he's from the nearby community, he shouldn't be trusted."

"Make anyone working for you take a lie detector test."

"Don't use local contractors; they'll cheat and steal."

"Build a wall."

That last piece of advice, disconcertingly reminiscent as it was of a certain political Leader's foreign policy at the time, pulled me up short. I was reminded of a stanza from "They Want Us to Be Afraid" by the Tehranian poet Kamand Kajouri. It reads:

> They want us to be afraid.
> They want us to be afraid of leaving our homes,
> to barricade our doors and hide our children.
> They aim to make us fear life!
>
> They want us to hate.
> They want us to hate the other,
> to practice aggression and perfect oppression.

They aim to divide us all!

This felt like the tale of two tales all over again—two conflicting paradigmatic world views. I could feel the influence of the old narrative, its story dominated by fear, control, and coercion. And I sensed the call of the new narrative, inviting us to imagine a story that could help to bridge this decades-old divide.

We desperately wanted the community to see that we were different, but precedence and history were not on our side. What reason did they have to trust us? Even Marco Antonio, who had kept his job and was now a member of the SERES team, didn't really consider us any different from his last employer. Here we were, more than three months in, and the only words he ever offered were a "Yes/no, ma'am," unerringly delivered to a point approximately one foot in front of his worn-out work boots, where he would dig intently in the dirt with the point of his ever-present machete.

If we wanted to have any hope of changing the situation, creating space for a new story to be told, we first had to prove ourselves trustworthy.

We'd intentionally put off designing the center before we found the right property because we knew we wanted the design to respond to the specifics of the place itself. Now that we'd purchased the land, it was one of the first activities on our list. With big dreams of sleeping accommodation, classrooms, demonstrative plots, renewable energy generation, a working farm, and a biodiversity conservation area, we knew this was no simple exercise. Our plan was to run a multi-day workshop on the property, including youth from across our programs as well as architects, agrologists, engineers, educators, and many others with specific expertise who would help enrich the process with their ideas and experiences.

A few days prior to the workshop, I walked the finca with Marco Antonio. Sweating profusely under the hot tropical sun, I explained as we went how we would set up different observation stations (yes, ma'am), where we'd keep supplies and workshop materials (yes, ma'am), and how we'd need to rig some temporary bathroom facilities (yes, ma'am). I also asked if he could invite a few local farmers, who could provide input on farming conditions. "Yes, ma'am," he assured the bare patch of soil at his feet.

Having finished our rounds, I climbed up into the pickup truck we had left parked under the shade of the old mango grove at the farm's entrance. The air hung thick and heavy with the scent of fermenting mangos. "There's one more thing," I called out to Marco Antonio, as I started the truck and gratefully switched on the air conditioning. "We have one person whose job will be to guide us through this whole process. Their role will be the most important really, they'll have to keep us grounded, tell us when we are getting off track, and bring us back to what is realistic: for this place, these communities."

"Yes, ma'am," said Marco Antonio, impaling a half-rotted mango seed on the point of his machete.

"That's you," I said. I smiled as I caught his confused stare and put the truck into reverse. "See you tomorrow, sir."

It took a lot of convincing from the rest of us on the team to persuade Marco Antonio that his knowledge of the local area would be invaluable to ensuring we came up with a design that would work, but we brought him around eventually. And a few weeks later, when he stood in front of a room full of educated professionals and told the two architects that, with all due respect, putting the building where they were proposing just wouldn't work, I knew we'd reached a project milestone more significant than completing a design or finishing a building ever would be. That moment was the beginning of a new story, a Weaving story, one Marco Antonio was helping us to shape. This would be a story about responsible land stewardship—done in partnership *with* the community—to foster connection, caring, and resilience. And it was a story whose validity was tested three years later, in June 2018, with the lethal eruption of nearby Volcán Fuego.

THE PHOENIX ARISES

Fuego Volcano, located about seven kilometers from our property, erupted on June 3, 2018. When it did so, it sent hot pyroclastic flows and heavy volcanic mudslides racing down its slopes. These lethal landslides buried homes, destroyed crops, wiped out infrastructure, and left hundreds dead and thousands displaced.

But the factors that had kept these communities and towns so marginalized for decades were not erased simply because a tragedy had occurred. This time the power divide was between the emergency humanitarian response and the people themselves: a poignant contrast between those whose lives and livelihoods were *made* in the disaster and those whose lives and livelihoods were *destroyed* in the disaster.

Emergency aid and the associated implementing partners and volunteers flooded into the country, drowning out local voices and local responses. Hotels in Escuintla, the nearest city to the disaster, were completely booked out, while halls and meeting rooms in the capital city overflowed with representatives from every well-known humanitarian organization that exists.

While those newly arrived experts debated for hours over which technology platform they would use to register the displaced communities in official shelters (which hadn't been built yet), Don Edgar stood in a long line outside the local primary school—temporarily converted into a morgue—attempting to solve a different problem. He was trying to work out how to get in and identify the remains of his loved ones. His thick, dark hair stood up at all angles, and he had smudges of black soot across his cheek and forehead.

The government bureaucrat sitting at the door was demanding a birth certificate for each of the deceased, and helpfully offering to print new ones—for fifty quetzales—for anyone that didn't have the required documents.

I walked up to him where he stood waiting towards the front of the line. "Don Edgar," I said, grasping his elbow in the way of greeting that is common in that part of the country. "What do you need? How can I support you?"

He glanced up, a haunted look on his face. "They were at mass," he said, "so at least they were ready to be taken to God."

I choked up immediately and grasped his elbow tighter. Don Edgar's wife and three daughters, along with a number of other community members, had been sitting in church when it was engulfed by the fast-moving pyroclastic flow.

"I was out in the field, working. Everything I own—my money, my identity card—was at home. And now it's gone." He looked back at the long line of people stretching behind him, then back to the government official, and, finally, back to me. I felt, as much as heard, his defeated sigh. "How can we possibly give them what they're asking for?" He shook his head as he glanced upward at the sky, which was gradually getting dark, before looking back at me, tears in his eyes and a look of desperation on his face. "We've been here since yesterday morning," he told me, "I have to see my wife and daughters. But I still have to find my son."

"It's okay," I told him, struggling with my own tears. "We'll find him."

Don Edgar's son was one of about one hundred and twenty SERES youth from the local area who we were determined to find and support through this tragic event. But it was chaotic. As we went from makeshift shelter to makeshift shelter—in people's homes, under hastily erected plastic sheeting, and rapidly converted community buildings—Don Edgar's desperate situation was just one of hundreds that we heard about.

We visited churches with people sleeping side-by-side on the floor, desperately short on food and basic hygiene items, while a hundred meters away a government-run donation shelter overflowed with inventory. We spoke to families denied access to help because the government had never acknowledged the existence of their community. Parents separated from their children, who didn't have any money to put credit on their phones to make a phone call and try to find them. And we received nonstop calls from people across Guatemala who had amassed donations and supplies who were desperate to help in some way.

As the days unfolded, we unapologetically leveraged our relationships and networks to help locate missing family members, reunite families, get food and medical supplies to hundreds of emergency makeshift shelters, deliver meals and clothing to people waiting outside the school-cum-morgue, and ensure local community leaders were considered and consulted in the government's recovery plans. We found ways for the large fincas to use their resources and infrastructure to support their neighbors. We even arranged for refrigerated trucks to be sent in to help the Red Cross in their temporary morgue, which without air conditioning was rapidly becoming untenable under the relentless heat of the tropical sun.

The whole time in the back of my mind, I kept wondering: *why us?* We were without a doubt the smallest, least resourced organization out here. Why were we delivering PPE to the Red Cross volunteers and coordinating with the army? But even as I asked the question, I knew the answer.

The aid-industrial complex—a monument to the patterns of old— was in full swing everywhere I turned, and there were countless moments during those long eighteen-to-twenty-hour days when I wasn't sure whether to weep or rage at the injustices being perpetuated on people who had already lost so much. As author and historian Rebecca Solnit writes in the foreword to her book *Hope in the Dark*, "The assumption behind much disaster response [...] is that civilization is a brittle façade, and behind it lies our true nature as monstrous, selfish, chaotic, and violent or as timid, fragile, and helpless."[1]

Every time I watched a volunteer proudly sporting a Fuego 2018 t-shirt take a selfie or heard someone ask for a photo as they handed over a pair of boots to a grieving parent, I wanted to walk away. But I knew I couldn't. Staying close even through the grief and despair was part of writing the new story. SERES'a proximity and intimate understanding of the affected communities, along with the credibility and trust we'd built, placed us in the unique position to bridge the divide and help get support to where it was most needed. So we did.

We continued to stay present and engaged, to push back against those sacrificing community and connection in their drive for efficiency, and to challenge the stereotypes that assumed these communities were unable to make decisions about their own welfare. And as the money dried up and the international spotlight moved on to the next disaster, we assured people we weren't going anywhere.

Searching together for ways to find meaning and dignity amongst the rubble and ruins, we emerged together stronger, more resilient, and, finally, ready to start writing a new story. One based on trust, connection, and caring, with a new, emergent vision for the SERES finca—renamed Finca Ulew, which means fire in Kaqchikel—that was so much more vibrant than what we, as an organization, could ever have imagined.

One of the difficulties of a people-driven, process-centric, place-based approach to creating change is that there isn't a neat beginning or end. It's ongoing, emergent. So how, then, do you tell that a new story is starting? Listen deeply. Pay attention. Feel its presence.

I heard whispers of that story in Sandra's parents, who buried the daughter they lost in the eruption in a coffin draped with her SERES Youth Ambassador t-shirt.

I saw signs of that story in Steven, another of SERES's Youth Ambassadors. He suffered third-degree burns to his legs and feet after running over hot volcanic mud to escape the eruption, only to run a marathon less than twelve months afterward to raise money for more youth leadership programs in the temporary encampment where he and hundreds of others still lived.

And I felt the strength of that story in Marco Antonio, sitting on the couch beside me at a team retreat, as we explored our roles and purpose within the evolution of the organization. When it was Marco Antonio's turn, he sat up straight, looked around at everyone, and said, "I'm going to be the director of the Finca." He threw his arm around me and looked me in the eyes. "*Coris* knows, don't you?" he said with a huge smile.

Coris. It makes me cringe, just a little. But still—it's the best nickname I've ever had.

SUMMARY

- Projects or programs that are not underpinned by a people, process, place philosophy (the three Weaver Lores) will never be truly sustainable or transformative.
- Local leaders don't just have skin-in-the-game, they have their lives on the line. When the going gets tough, they aren't going anywhere.
- Building trust takes time, particularly when working with people for whom the social contract has not worked.

EXERCISE:

1. The Weaving Lores.

People, process, place. These are the three Weaving Lores. They take a bit of practice to recognize. Take a highlighter and read back through the last two sections—No More Walls, and The Phoenix Arises—and mark all of the different places where you see one or more of these Lores applied. How was it different from a business-as-usual scenario? How do you think that this might have impacted the short, medium and long-term change?

CHAPTER 10
SEVEN STRATEGIES FOR EFFECTIVE WEAVING

 "Come to the edge," he said.
"We can't, we're afraid!" they responded.
"Come to the edge," he said.
"We can't, We will fall!" they responded.
"Come to the edge," he said.
And so they came.
And he pushed them.
And they flew.

— GUILLAUME APOLLINAIRE

In Part I of *The Weaver's Way*, we discussed the idea that stories and narratives can have a very influential role in the way we live our lives. We also talked about how the existing Western narratives may have embedded deep in our cultural psyche certain beliefs about who has the power, permission, position, and perspective for shaping change. We concluded Part I by proposing that it's time for a different story—or for a collection of stories—called We, The Weavers. And that within this collection, there existed a story about how each and every one of us could more proactively engage with creating change in our sphere of influence to collectively contribute towards making the world a better place.

In Part II, we then examined *The Weaver's Way* framework. This framework gave us the building blocks for these new stories, guiding principles and ideas for ways in which we can approach shaping change to ensure that it is more meaningful and transformative.

We now know about the five guiding principles and three Weaving Lores that make up The Weaver's Way—a framework for shaping change that is meaningful and transformative. This is not a theoretical framework. It's a framework for taking action and, as I mentioned at the start of Part II, for it to have any significant impact it needs you, dear Reader. To test it out. To try it on. To play with it and make it *yours*.

In this chapter, I've put together seven strategies—tips, if you will —to help you as you begin your Weaving Practice. As in the other chapters, I've included stories about lessons I've learned and mistakes I've made in my own practice that might help you in yours. And I've included one more person I'd like you to meet from the Weaver's Guild.

I hope you keep coming back to this chapter as you go out and begin Weaving. The questions posed assume you're already working on intentionally shaping change in some capacity and are framed to help you reflect on those efforts. Even if you are just starting out, however, they're useful. Just tweak the questions so they work for your particular circumstance.

STRATEGY I: HOW TO PREVENT KNOTS

I watched Loida prepare to weave. She brought out her loom, her stool, a basket of yarn, and what looked like a worrying tangle of sticks and threads. I thought of my half-hearted attempts at knitting when I was young. The brightly colored ball of wool wound so neatly and inviting. Until I started knitting, that is. Then somehow, it got away from me and rolled off the couch and across the living room floor. I gathered it back up, trying to rewind it into some semblance of order. But as I wedged it safely between the sofa cushions and took up my knitting needles once again, I could already see it happening: another discarded project, thwarted by a big, messy knot that felt too challenging to try to disentangle.

I shared with Loida this sorry story of my half-finished, abandoned projects as she continued to unpack her things.

Then she turned to me. "Half-finished?" she asked with a small smile. "It sounds like you never actually started." Behind her, a small transformation has occurred. The corner of the patio, with its wooden post, rusty nails, and assortment of chickens clucking and scratching was now a weaver's workshop, tools and materials neatly laid out and ready to be used. She turned back, took a seat, and began to weave.

Her comments made me think about what it means to prepare ourselves properly for the process of shaping change. Would better preparation, as Loida demonstrated, help us in our work as Weavers? I reflected back on the knots, often painful, that have caught me up in my own journey. I also reflected on conversations with friends and clients, enmeshed in messy and often emotionally distressing situations, distracting them from their work. It seems there are at least a few common threads to those snarls.

The first has to do with believing you *do* have the permission, power, perspective, and position to shape change. For many of us, those without a leading role, the old narrative makes us question our self-value and self-worth when it comes to putting our ideas into action. How many times, I wonder, has self-doubt stopped me from speaking up, taking a stand, or engaging in action that I knew was the right thing to do? Or blanketed me in a miasma of shame and humiliation after I did so? Too many to count. But as I've built my identity as a Weaver, I've witnessed a quiet transformation taking place. Deep in my core, a conviction is building, its whispered voice a strong counterpoint to the poisonous self-doubt. *You are here. You belong. You're part of this Weaving story.*

Let me assure you, dear reader, so are you.

The second thread often responsible for those ugly knots has to do with integrity. When a tapestry or fabric loses its integrity, it loses its strength and functionality: the ability to fulfill the purpose for which it was designed. Weavers work to shape change in support of the collective well-being of people and the planet over time, and *The Weaver's Way* framework is designed to help us do that. The guiding principles are a Weaver's proverbial integrity yardstick. The times when I have not been true to these principles have been the times when I have tripped and fallen the hardest.

Learning to work with integrity requires aligning our thoughts, feelings, and intentions with our words and actions. As you become more aware of this alignment, you'll also find your ability to listen for integrity is sharpened. I experience this as an intuitive *sensing*, deep inside. I think, "Something about this situation/person is a little *off*." I refer to this as my *spidey senses*. Whenever I meet someone or hear someone speak that is not in alignment, these spidey sensors light up —something I've found occurring all too often lately when listening to our elected Leaders on the evening news.

Use the guiding principles as your compass. If you're in doubt, or need to evaluate a particular situation, they can help you. Also, get used to listening for integrity. Turn on and tune in your spidey senses (or whatever name you wish to give them) and pay attention. When your senses are singing they are telling you there's more to be discovered here!

The third and final thread that often tangles us up relates to the stories themselves. In a world where being nice seems to have become the only acceptable moral virtue, it can be difficult to go against the flow. But stepping into a new narrative requires us to do just that, like our Weavers Patty Curran or Joyce Yee. Author and organizational psychologist Adam Grant described these kinds of people in his book, *Originals*, as "disagreeable givers" or individuals who are skeptical and challenging of the status quo but ultimately committed to the greater good. These disagreeable givers, argues Grant, tend to be the best change agents.[1]

Being a nonconformist is not something that comes naturally to everyone. And there is a definite gender bias against women who were raised to be nice little girls. Like I was. I learned from a young age that rocking the boat had dangerous consequences, and I've had to work hard to feel confident singing out of tune to the choir.

What has helped me over the years become a more confident disagreeable giver is to adopt the mantra "kind, not nice." When I recognize the old stories and patterns at play, I've learned to know when and how to say no to them with kindness and compassion. It's not always easy, but I'm strengthened by the knowledge that the alternative I'm proposing is in service of a better future for all.

This mantra also helps me remember that blame and shame have no place here. We were born into these old stories, often without our choosing. What we *can* choose is to have the courage and determination to leave the old stories behind and write a brave new story.

EXERCISES

1. Becoming a Weaver is about reclaiming your privilege to shape change.
Prepare yourself for the work of Weaving by building this identity. Try it on. Get familiar with how it invites you to act, react, and interact. Welcome it in and give it a place to sit comfortably alongside your other identities. Tell yourself: I do have the power, permission, position, and perspective to shape change. I am here. I belong. I am part of this Weaving story.

2. Are you clear on your purpose?
Ask yourself: Why is the change I'm working toward important? Then,

scan through and check that your thoughts, feelings, intentions, words, and actions are aligned with that purpose.

3. Practice using the guiding principles as your integrity yardstick. Choose a recent situation or event as an example and go over the five principles. Ask yourself: How is tension and conflict used here? Does it feel safe and constructive or threatening and destructive? What of the main actors? Are we/they working with humility, or driven by ego? Are we being curious, or quick to judge? Are we rigid in our thinking/planning/approach or nimble and agile? Are we being time-full? Or time-scarce? Make a note of any areas where you believe some adjustment may be needed to better align with the guiding principles.

STRATEGY 2: CHOOSE YOUR LOOM

The type of loom, the quality and color of the threads, the style of weaving, all these decisions are determined by considering the final product that a weaver desires to make. In this way *form* will always follow *function*. The same should be true of Weaving. A Weaver grounds themselves first in being clear on their purpose and the outcomes they are hoping to achieve before deciding what structures and/or processes to use.

I say *should* because it's surprising to me how often we operate on autopilot, unquestioningly using the same form and format time and again even when the purpose and outcomes we're hoping for are very different. This can be for something as simple as a meeting (how many of us default to an hour-long meeting, irrespective of the people and topics proposed?) or as complex as an organizational structure. Choosing the right form for doing your work will have a significant impact on your ability to shape transformative change. To borrow from the title of feminist author and civil rights activist Audre Lorde's most famous essay, titled "The Master's Tools Will Never Dismantle the Master's House."[2]

I've already shared a few examples in this book. Like the logical framework—a tool developed for military purposes that is now being used for development projects—that I discussed in Chapter 8. But to illustrate how important this idea is, let me share another, more personal and painful example from SERES's startup years.

This was a time early on during SERES's startup years, when we were trying to build up our board of directors. In most countries, a board of directors is a standard legal requirement for any registered organization. We'd started SERES with a board of directors composed of eight of our Youth Ambassadors who had been most active within the organization.

But as a fledgling nonprofit, we were struggling to make ends meet. We were also getting a lot of questions from foundation officers who wanted to know who our board members were (and who were often dissatisfied with what they found). The advice I kept on receiving was that we needed to get a fundraising board, and so we did. Consequently, our board members quickly transitioned to being (with all the best intentions) white, well-connected folks who did not live in Central America.

But while this meant we could tick the required boxes on grant applications and finally satisfy those interested with our "good governance," it didn't feel right. We discussed it among the board members at length until we became convinced it was about local leaders. Actually, Leaders. If we could get one or two people onto the board from some of the country's wealthy elite families, it would be a game changer. And it was—just not in the way we had anticipated.

I shared with the team my excitement for getting some well-connected local Leaders as board members, along with the names of a couple of new contacts I had just made whom we were thinking could be good candidates.

Straight away, Antonio warned me against it. "Those family names," he told me, "people know them. They played a significant role in the war, and not on the same side as the communities we work with. If we do this, people might question what we stand for."

But I refused to be dissuaded. Instead, I defaulted back to the influence of urgency, passionately trying to persuade Antonio that this was the perfect opportunity to build a bridge over that historical divide and work together to heal the country.

In my own defense, I truly believed what I said, and as a board we were thrilled when we welcomed two new board members—one from Guatemala, one from El Salvador—into the SERES family. I felt even more triumphant when just a few weeks later I called to tell Antonio that thanks to one of our new board members, he now had a new suite of office furniture. The board member's father was remodeling his offices, and he could have whatever he wanted. I gave him the address where he could pick it up and, feeling a little smug, hung up the phone.

A few hours later, I came back from a meeting to see I had a number of missed calls from Antonio. Certain he'd been calling to tell me about how great the new office looked, I called him back, a smile already on my face.

But when he answered the phone, he was anything but happy. His voice was shaking and full of emotion, but I couldn't place what it was.

"What's happened?" I asked, my own voice full of concern.

Antonio had made arrangements with the board member to go to her father's offices to pick up the furniture. She wouldn't be there, she'd said, but everything was arranged. He just needed to talk to the secretary and then load on what they wanted. He'd asked one of our Youth Ambassadors to help him out.

They borrowed a pickup truck, and the two of them set out, driving the hour and a half into the capital where they quickly passed into another world: full of the tree-lined boulevards, sprawling malls, and luxury condominiums that define San Salvador's wealthy suburbs. All was going to plan, he told me.

They'd spoken with the secretary and then started to load furniture into the truck when a large SUV with darkened windows pulled up beside them. Three heavily armed security guards all pointing handguns got out, followed by a man who started screaming at Antonio and his friend.

"He was so angry," said Antonio, "he wouldn't stop yelling, and all the while we had guns pointed at our heads. I tried to explain the situation and asked him to call his daughter. But he just wouldn't listen. He just kept screaming that we were thieves." He paused for a moment, obviously still shaken.

I was also upset at what had happened, but it was his next words that broke my heart.

"I've been robbed and held up before," he told me, "and I'm used to violence. It's not about being afraid. But he made me feel that because I—we—were poor, we were nothing, not even allowed to speak and defend ourselves, not even worthy of being heard. I've never been so humiliated in my life."

I felt sick to my stomach. "I'm so sorry, Antonio," I told him, tears running down my cheeks. "I'll make it up to you."

There was silence on the other end of the phone. "That man took away my dignity," he told me quietly. "I'm not here for this." And hung up the phone.

But what could I do? I called the board member and explained what had happened (she never returned Antonio's calls).

"Don't worry about it," she said breezily, making me wonder if she thought I was trying to apologize for what had happened. "We all get a little angry sometimes. Antonio can just come back tomorrow and get it."

I tried to explain that what'd happened was about much more than some donated furniture. Antonio needed to be seen and heard, I told her. He deserved, at the very least, an apology. The conversation ended with a half-hearted promise to call Antonio (which never happened), and that absence quickly turned into a general radio silence for all things SERES-related. I guess we'd become a problem that was easier ignored.

How did this go so wrong that the cofounder of SERES came so close to stepping away—or being taken away?

How? Because *form* had become more important than *function*.

The board of directors—at least in its traditional form—is a structure that's very much a legacy of the colonial and patriarchal structures of the old narrative, where board members represented a small social class at the top of a rigid hierarchy. And nowhere was this model more true than in Central America, with its oligarchy and ruling elite.

I had taken the master's tools and without realizing it, downloaded El Salvador's historic power struggles into our organizational DNA just as quickly and effectively as clicking on a flashing popup advising you've won the lottery will download a Trojan horse onto your hard drive. The damage was just as devastating.

The saving grace of that painful lesson was it took us down a long, circuitous road of inquiry to discover what it meant for us as an organization to reimagine this concept of "board of directors," and create something built from new patterns, not old ones. We asked ourselves: How does this form (the board of directors) serve our function?

We challenged traditional board language (such as *oversee* and *ensure*) that implied a lack of trust in competency and capability and instead elevated language that stood true to our values. We talked about whose voice it was important to center and how to elevate that voice to ensure it was heard. We changed structures from committees to circles and made those circles spaces for generating productive tension and dialogue, rather than agreement and certainty.

And what emerged from that process was a multilingual, multi-generational group whose roles were to be stewards, system sensors, and resources for SERES, and who were elected and affirmed each year by SERES Youth Ambassadors themselves. We found the loom that was right for us.

Whether it's deciding on an organizational structure, developing a meeting agenda, or choosing activities for a workshop it pays to stop and check—are these the master's tools, as Audre Lorde would call them? Too often, the conventional structures, tools, and practices used to organize how we work together stifle inclusion and engagement. Just like our stories, they need to change.

I've shared a few different examples in this book—the co-leadership model, SERES's organizational structure, as well as the organizations run by the Weavers from the Weaver's Guild). I've also added a few more resources in the More Information section, where you can find other ideas for structures, tools, and practices that are more aligned with a new Weaver story.

EXERCISES

1. WHAT ARE THE STRUCTURES, TOOLS, AND PRACTICES YOU USE TO DO YOUR WORK?

What are their origins? What is their purpose? Do you feel they bring you closer to your values, or further away from them?

2. STOP AND REFLECT.

We're often trained to go straight from problem to action, grabbing the tool that's closest to hand. But it pays to stop and reflect. Ask yourself: What are the needs of the different groups of people who will be involved in this process? What is the purpose or goal of this work? What are our shared objectives? Once you have that clear, you can think about which tool to use.

STRATEGY 3: DON'T OVERPOWER, EMPOWER

If you recall from earlier in the book, one of the aspects that makes the backstrap loom so unique is that it requires the weaver to bind herself into the loom and use her body to create the required tension for weaving. There is a beautiful poetry to the physical and existential nature of this arrangement: the loom cannot exist without the weaver and the weaver cannot *be* without the loom. It also provides a wonderful image to understand the way that power is used in The Weaver's Way framework and how this differs from the old approach.

The old narrative—the Game—is one based on separateness, upheld through the scaffolding of power structures that require power to be held *over* another. In this old narrative, power is a zero-sum game. If I have more, you have less. The aim of the Game is a steady accumulation of power through domination, coercion, and control.

And it is antithetical to the The Weaver's Way framework. A weaver does not—indeed cannot—use coercion and control to dominate the loom. To do so would be to control and dominate herself. On the flip side of this—and one I encounter quite often when working with groups that have been marginalized or oppressed—is the rejection of all power as a form of bad or evil. But again, a weaver cannot give up and deny all power. This would collapse the loom and in doing so, reject her own existence.

So how does a weaver use power? The weaver uses power in a way that is fluid and dynamic, seeking to *express* rather than *oppress* to fulfill her purpose. She gives power to the loom while at the same time receiving it, creating power both with and within in a seamless and continuous exchange.

To use power in this way we must first recognize there are many sources of power, which our different identities give us access to. This is why creating ease and familiarity with our multiplicity of identities is so important. It allows us to move in and out of these sources of power rather than clinging desperately to something that feels like a scarce resource.

The list below based on the Rockwood Institute's Art of Leadership training lists some of the most common sources of power used in contemporary Western society. As you look through the list, you'll probably recognize that some of these sources of power have been favored by the old narrative as a means for exerting control and dominance. Other sources lend themselves more naturally to helping build power with, and power to. I don't believe, however, that any are exclusive to a particular narrative.

Personal power	Obstructive power
Co-power	Ideological power
Collaborative power	Institutional power
Positional power	Structural power
Expert power	Economic power
Cultural power	Transcendent power
Referred power	

There is great potential for innovation and creativity when we look into how we can adapt some of the traditional forms of power into *The Weaver's Way* framework, such as finding ways to make our institutions more inclusive or our economic systems more regenerative.

EXERCISES

1. WHAT IS YOUR RELATIONSHIP TO POWER IN YOUR WORK?
Go through the sources of power list. As you review each one, make a mark (✓) if it is a source of power you consciously use to do your work. Make another mark (!) if it is a source of power you encounter that hinders your work. As power over or power with and within?

2. ARE YOU PREPARED TO SURRENDER TO THE LOOM?
For a Weaver to use power it must flow. Can you identify where you're holding on to certain sources of power and let go, trusting it will be returned to you when you need it?

3. Strengthen your ability to shape change by becoming more agile and fluid: giving and receiving in a seamless and continuous exchange. Go back over the sources of power list, and for each one listed ask yourself: How might I use this source of power intentionally to create the change I'm working on? Next, ask yourself: How might I give this power away to someone else in service to their work of shaping change?

STRATEGY 4: FIND THE RHYTHM OF THE WEAVE

Shortly after I met Abigail back in 2010, she came to participate in a week-long leadership training Antonio and I were hosting with about a dozen other young leaders from across Guatemala and El Salvador. After dinner one evening, we all gathered together in the living room (which was really just an office space we'd filled with brightly covered, oversized cushions). These "between" times at our trainings are precious and intentional, as shared laughter and storytelling lay the foundations for deep friendship and connection.

On this particular evening, the theme that'd emerged was about rituals and traditions—some from childhood but many still a part of daily community life. I learned about different ways to ward off the evil eye (generally involving a lot of spitting), listened to warnings about what will happen to the cow if you let her milk boil over (she'll become covered in blisters), and winced at the painful-sounding rituals that young man went through to ensure they developed strong pectoral muscles (I can no longer look at a bull ant without cringing).

I listened and laughed, surprised more at the similarities than the differences between my own childhood and theirs. But while the daily minutiae of childhood trials and tribulations may have been familiar, I was curious about something else. The broader context that existed as each of us passed from children to adults and how it may have influenced the way each of us showed up as we gathered together here in this room.

When it came to my turn to ask, I shifted the conversation slightly toward a question that had been on my mind for some time. "Each of you was born at the end of what were decades-long societal conflicts in your respective countries. Civil war, essentially," I said. "So I'm curious. How'd that affect you growing up?"

One by one, their answers came back:

The war didn't affect me, because our family fled to Honduras where we lived as refugees until I was nine...

The war didn't affect me, just my two uncles who were taken by government forces and we never found out what happened...

The same story was repeated again and again around the circle. "The War Didn't Affect Me" could easily become the title of a collection of stories about unacknowledged intergenerational trauma.

The war didn't affect me because when I was four, there was a massacre in the town square in a community across the lake from ours. From that moment on, my parents made sure we knew how important it was to stay silent and not speak out so we would be safe.

This final, heartbreaking story was delivered in a quiet voice by Abigail, who was always the last to speak up.

From the time I'd met Abigail she'd always presented with a timorous demeanor, shy and reserved and generally reluctant to express herself in any setting with more than three or four people. Just the day before she'd come up to me following that afternoon's session, distressed and uncomfortable, and apologetically tried to explain that the reason she didn't speak up wasn't for a lack of interest. "I don't know what's wrong with me," she said, "I want to share, but I can't get the words out. By the time I feel ready, a few hours have gone by and the moment has gone."

As I listened to her share her "The War Didn't Affect Me" story, I had goosebumps.

This is what Loida means when she talks about patience. Patience doesn't mean idleness or complacency. Every weaving has its own rhythm, and our job as Weavers is to discover it. This is the essence of Timefullness. You cannot rush healing. You cannot rush the building of trust. And the reality is that a Weaver's work will always involve these two things.

The intergenerational trauma spoken of in our living room that evening wasn't unique to those who were gathered there. The sad truth is that the old narratives of patriarchy, colonization, and extractivism have caused trauma for many of us.

One of the most useful definitions of trauma I've come across is the following: *trauma is any event or set of events that occurred in your life that made you think the world was unsafe, that broke your trust in people that you're surrounded by, that really caused you to just not trust.*

Trauma is different for everyone, but I know for most of the individuals and groups who I've worked with over the years—people who've been systematically marginalized and oppressed, internally displaced persons and political refugees—the breakdown in trust wasn't only interpersonal but systemic. The social contract itself had failed them and in many ways continued to do so. What reason did they have to think that this time it would be any different?

After hearing Abigail's story, we returned to that moment time and again over the years. Whether it was in academic, professional, or private settings, there wasn't one aspect of her life unaffected by that event she'd described. She struggled in a lecture theatre, at conferences, and sitting around the dinner table with my own family, always wrestling with that question: *if she let herself be seen and heard in this moment, could she trust the world to keep her safe?*

This created tension with an outside world that needed to wave a magic wand and have Abigail suddenly be "empowered," ready to inspire us with her story of overcoming adversity.

But that isn't how it works. We had to work in such a way that allowed Abigail to cultivate the courage and bravery to reconnect those broken threads. We had to move at the speed of trust.

EXERCISES

1. TRUST IS THE CURRENCY OF SOCIAL CAPITAL, AND SOCIAL CAPITAL IS WHAT WE'LL NEED TO BUILD TO TRULY FIND OUR WAY IN AN INTERCONNECTED AND INTERDEPENDENT WORLD.

How's your piggy bank faring? Are you spending your money on bonds or bridges? What kinds of things could you do to start building up your trust bank?

2. WHENEVER YOU BEGIN WORKING WITH ANY NEW INDIVIDUAL, COMMUNITY, OR GROUP, STOP AND ASK YOURSELF: WHO AM I TO THESE PEOPLE?

Which parts of who I am may inspire trust and what parts distrust? What will it take to become trustworthy?

STRATEGY 5: EMBRACE EMERGENCE

One of the things I love most about weaving as a metaphor for shaping change is how beautifully it reminds us to embrace emergence. Emergence, the beautiful complexity that arises from a multiplicity of seemingly simple interactions. Like water molecules transforming into snowflakes, meristematic cells producing the wonderful Romanesco broccoli, or a collection of colorful threads becoming a vibrant tapestry.

The importance of emergence cannot be underestimated when it comes to shaping change, yet it receives remarkably little attention in our change narratives. We airbrush it out in the recounting of our success stories because it undermines the linear hero narrative.

Perhaps this is because emergence, by its very nature, requires us to let go of certainty, in stark contrast to the command-and-control thinking of old. Remember Therese Caouette trying to teach her students to "be in the moment"? To embrace emergence is to acknowledge the twists and turns then find the courage to take action despite the fact we cannot control the outcome.

Perhaps this is what inspired Aristotle (one of the first to write about emergence) to remark that "courage is the first of human qualities." But even as we embrace emergence and accept the unpredictable and contingent nature of a Weaver's work, we don't have to rely on courage alone. There are a few techniques that can help us get closer to the final outcome.

First, focus on the process, not just the final product. Weaving is done line by line, the weft weaving in and out of the warp, each action a union of *intention* and *attention*. A Weaver creates opportunities for people to come together and generate solutions. Build care and connection, work with a humble heart, and as a young Kaquikel friend of mine told me as she was learning to weave: *If you make an error, no matter how far along you are, simply go back to where you made the mistake and fix it. You cannot keep weaving as though it didn't happen because you will always know, whenever you look at it, that the error is there.*

Second: The Weaver's Way framework is intended to be like a compass rather than a map. Weaving is not the same as a color-by-number cross-stitch with easy-to-follow instructions and a glossy photo you can look at for guidance. In this kind of Weaving, your sense of purpose is like a North Star that shows you the direction you are headed, but you must look for the patterns and landmarks as they emerge to guide your steps. It's a concept known as na k'am ruach in Tzutujil.

Na k'am ruach is how you weave, explains Loida. *There is no paper or canvas with the designs already recorded. You learn from those that have gone before you, you become inspired by the world around you, and you hold in your heart and your mind an idea of what you are working toward. The colors of the sky, the flowers, the animals, all of these speak to us. And so the painter paints pictures of the lake, the harvest, the market; the weaver embroiders the birds, the mountains. Everything we do is na k'am ruach, extracted, adapted, replicated from something else. Then, when you start weaving, although you have an idea of what you want, it's about doing it and seeing it. Every thread counts. You need to know how to see each one, see how their contribution will get the patterns and shapes that you want.*

Finally, with the humility and curiosity that are essential attitudes of the Weaver, learn to ask powerful questions without knowing the answers. Learning to use questions in this way helps us to develop what author Thomas Schwandt refers to as an "evaluating mindset," curious and inquisitive, reflective, self-critical, and open-minded—all essential qualities for embracing emergence. Over time, you will learn to develop a deep love for the questions themselves. I experience a frisson of excitement whenever someone asks me a powerful question, as my imagination shoots off into so many different directions. Answers, after all, lie in the past. And our job is to call forth the future.

EXERCISES

Loida speaks of paying attention, listening deeply, and tuning in to a way of knowing that is more sensing than thinking. Reflective practices such as meditation, prayer, or mindfulness as well as creative pursuits like journaling or sketching can be helpful ways to tune in.

1. WHAT TOOLS OR TECHNIQUES MIGHT YOU TRY TO QUIET YOUR THINKING MIND and tune in to the patterns of perception, thought, and action emerging around you? Make a list of all of the different activities you think might be helpful or that you're curious to try. Now choose one, go out and try it.

2. ARE YOU LEADING WITH A QUESTION OR AN ANSWER? Come up with a North Star question for something you are working on or care about, but make sure you don't know the answer! Make your question bold and curious. Write it down, then go out and explore the unknown. See where it takes you.

STRATEGY 6: PAY ATTENTION TO THE EDGES

THERE IS AN ECOLOGICAL CONCEPT MANY SUSTAINABLE GARDENERS WOULD BE familiar with known as the edge effect. The edge effect describes how there is always a greater diversity of life in the edges where two ecosystems overlap, such as land/water or forest/grassland. The same is true of human ecosystems.

There is a richness at the edges that is too often overlooked. People at the margins are so often seen as the beneficiaries of change processes but rarely the engines of change. Yet when it comes to resilience, adaptation, resourcefulness—all qualities we will need in spades in the not-too-distant future—there is no better place to look than toward the people living in the places where the only option is to solve the problems that matter. These voices on the fringes hold many of the answers to our greatest challenges.

Strategy 6 also carries a word of warning.

"Pay attention to the edges," Loida said on more than one occasion. "They are what gives the fabric strength. If you let them become torn and frayed, it unravels."

It's a truth the COVID-19 pandemic demonstrated all too well, as renowned author and thinker Malcolm Gladwell was quick to point out to thousands of U.S. healthcare professionals in June of 2020. He used the opportunity to urge a change in the healthcare system. Rather than continuing to invest in high-end teaching hospitals and specialized physician training, he urged healthcare needed to look to the edges and invest resources into the margins such as in low-income communities that cannot afford or access coverage. Failure to do this, according to Gladwell, was one of the reasons why the pandemic had such devastating consequences for a country that had previously been ranked as the most prepared nation for withstanding just such an event.

This is an ongoing theme for Gladwell. A few years earlier, in a podcast titled "My Little Hundred Million," Gladwell had argued that Western society had gone too far in what he referred to as the strong link paradigm: continued investment into the best, the brightest, the fastest—AKA the Leaders and heroes of old.[3] As a result, the inequality gap grew, and the edges became more frayed, creating the preexisting condition with which we entered the pandemic. And so the unraveling was accelerated, the margins became wider, our fabric more fragile.

EXERCISES

1. Where are your edges in your work?
Are they strong or weak and fraying? What needs to be done to strengthen and restore those edges?

2. Who or what lies at the margins in your community or work?
What might they be able to tell you about the change you are working on? What experience or wisdom do they hold? And how might you begin to include this in your work?

STRATEGY 7: ATTEND, MEND, REPAIR

In late 2015, nine months after the breakdown in the truce agreement between El Salvador's government and the country's main gangs, we hosted another leadership retreat for young community leaders from across Guatemala and El Salvador. Violence and murders in El Salvador were undergoing a horrifying resurgence, and we were particularly concerned about young men in our network like Wilbur, who you met in Chapter 1. The conflict had pushed out to previously peaceful rural areas, marked by an alarming seventy percent rise in murder rates, and many of the young men we worked with suddenly found themselves trapped between gang violence and state abuse; pawns in a battle they had little control over.

Our goal with the retreat was to give people a safe space to take a step back and reconnect, reflect, and recharge. We knew they were walking a delicate tightrope: By showing initiative and demonstrating leadership, SERES's Youth Ambassadors could be seen as a threat, and we wanted them to know they had our support, whether that meant leaning in and continuing to work or temporarily stepping back.

Sometime after dinner on the third night of the retreat, one of the young men came to tell us that another participant, Dereik, had disappeared. He'd been distant all day and acting a little strangely. In the afternoon, he'd drawn some lines and shapes onto his face, which everyone had joked about at the time. Then toward the end of dinner he'd said an emotional goodbye to the group and left the table.

"Everyone thought he'd gone back to the dorm," they told us. "But when a couple of us went to look, we couldn't find him."

Alarmed, Antonio and I headed out, and after about an hour of searching we found Dereik a few kilometers away. He was walking along the road with his backpack slung over his shoulder heading toward the intercity bus terminal. It took some persuading, but we finally managed to convince him to come back with us to discuss what had happened.

Sitting in the kitchen of my tiny one-room apartment (an extension of our small family-style retreat complex), Dereik explained to us that right before he'd left to come here, a gang had seized his younger brother, which he'd confirmed with his family. Through a series of text messages they told him he had three days to join the gang or his brother would be killed.

As Dereik understood it, he was facing a mutually exclusive choice: He couldn't belong to a gang and also be a member of SERES (which many of our youth referred to as their second family). He expected his peers and us as an organization to ostracize and incriminate him and so was rejecting us before we'd had a chance to reject him. And to be honest, he could hardly be blamed for this thinking.

Mainstream media and public narrative had created a very black-and-white image of the complex socio-political crisis, directing nothing but animosity and hatred toward anyone and anything connected to the gangs. There was no room in this story for the fact that many of those caught up in the tragic events were simply innocent bystanders, guilty of little more than poverty and circumstance. And as a result of this binary ultimatum, young people like Dereik, faced with an impossible decision, were suddenly cut off, alone, and isolated, vulnerable to ever more exploitation and marginalization. It was another single story, one that was ripping El Salvadoran society to shreds just as much as the violence itself.

Why do we insist on such oversimplified binaries when the world is so inherently paradoxical? Is this the result of a society that too easily accepts its people and the planet as disposable that we are so ready to discard that which we perceive as broken or damaged?

I remember once going to visit Abigail at her parents' house at the lake. I walked in, and there was Loida, sitting on her stool on the patio with a basket of clothing beside her and a pair of pants on her lap. Not weaving. Mending. Almost unconsciously, my toes curled up as though trying to disassociate themselves from the holes they normally poked out of. Thank goodness for my sneakers for hiding that pitiful state of affairs. Needless to say, mending socks—or any article of clothing, for that matter—is not my forte.

But while I place very little emphasis on my darning abilities, as a Weaver I've invested significant energy into learning to attend, mend, and repair—skills I believe will be in increasingly high demand in the near future.

We live in a world that is increasingly divided, fed on a constant diet of false dichotomies and facing an epidemic of loneliness and depression. A world where shame, blame, and accusations have become the tools for interaction, and conflict becomes a battle rather than an opportunity. A world like Dereik's.

This world needs Weavers. Weavers who can strengthen the social fabric and repair the broken threads that separate us from each other, and the world around us. Weavers who can hold us together against the forces that would tear us asunder. Weavers who know how to attend, mend, and repair.

Close to 11 p.m., we asked the participants to gather once again. There, seated in a circle on the floor of our living room, we asked Dereik to share what he'd told us. The initial reaction, not surprisingly, was one of anger. As we'd heard over the last few days, we knew that more than a few of the youth from El Salvador had lost friends and family members to the gangs, and they all lived in constant fear. It wasn't hard to see why Dereik had left rather than face this from his friends.

"You've betrayed us," came the angry words, the pain writ large on their upset faces. "You betrayed our family."

A tear is repaired by restoring the vital connections that have been severed. We must first see the individual threads and acknowledge the brokenness. Then we can begin strengthening, building, and renewing. For over four hours, Antonio and I worked to do what had been done so infrequently in regards to El Salvador's gang crisis—hold a space for sustained, respectful dialogue where people could be seen and heard. Round and round we went until the early hours of the morning, probing and questioning, listening and reflecting, allowing the group to find their way forward to a new story. One that included them all.

That new story, so different to mainstream media, acknowledged Dereik had very little choice. It also acknowledged family is a bond that's not easily broken. And it affirmed that this SERES family was one built on deep caring and connection, mutual respect, and trust. Dereik was offered a path to do what he must, knowing he would always be welcome with understanding and compassion back to the SERES family.

He went, but about eighteen months later was able to leave the gang and return to a normal life. Instead of ending up as one more grim statistic, he now lives with his family on the border between Guatemala and El Salvador, has a steady job, and is training as a youth facilitator to work with other vulnerable youth. His brother was unharmed.

EXERCISES

1. Do you have relationships that impact your work that need mending or repairing?
What is holding you back from addressing those tears? What could you do to start to heal the broken connections?

2. Are there any us/them binary stories creating division and separation in your community?
Where do these stories come from and who do they serve? Can you help to reframe the situation to create a different story?

These seven strategies are designed to help you become more adept both at being a Weaver, and the work of Weaving itself. As mentioned at the start of Part II, these two concepts are mutually inclusive, self-reinforcing, and regenerative. They belong together, one and the same. And when you have the opportunity to see it and experience it firsthand it is, quite simply, breathtaking.

It's time to meet Akaya Windwood.

WEAVER: AKAYA WINDWOOD

Akaya Windwood is a leadership development professional who has spent the majority of her career working to elevate the effectiveness of leadership and collaboration in the nonprofit and social benefit sectors. Although I didn't meet Akaya until 2017, the influence of her work had reached me years before when I trained at the Rockwood Leadership Institute, the U.S.'s largest provider of transformative leadership trainings for nonprofits, for which Akaya was the CEO for fourteen years.

In 2017 at a summit in Mexico for social change leaders, I had the first opportunity to witness Akaya in action. It was a sticky October evening, and I was sitting with two hundred or so other people under the bright stars at a beachside resort in Ixtapa, waiting for the event to kick off. After a few remarks from the MC, Akaya was invited to give the official welcome.

To the shouts and applause of a crowd of people who obviously knew and loved her, she stepped on stage. A tall, Black woman with tightly curled gray hair, wearing shorts and a t-shirt and no shoes, Akaya was as far from the image of an opening-night keynote speaker as one could imagine.

Before I'd even made the connection to Rockwood, listening to her give her welcoming words and watching her move through the crowd, stopping to say hello or give a hug, I knew I was observing something unusual. I had a sense I was witnessing someone incredibly powerful and influential, but with none of the usual trappings that those qualities implied. I had spent enough time among influential politicians, successful business Leaders, and the wealthy ruling class to know that *this* wasn't *that*. There was something different at play here. So... what was it exactly? I had to find out.

The opportunity to satisfy my curiosity came the following year when I was invited back to the summit, this time as one of the two dozen or so moderators. To my delight, Akaya was our guide, and—while intermittent—working with and getting to know Akaya over these past years has been a rich and rewarding experience, full of unexpected gifts.

Gifts, like those kinds of conversations that generate new ideas and insights that leave you ruminating for hours or even days afterward. Or being able to see an old problem from a completely new perspective. But perhaps the most precious of the gifts I've received from this relationship is faith. Not of the religious kind, but faith that when we turn away from the old narrative, when we commit ourselves to living into and breathing a new story, change is not only possible, but the world on the other side of that change is a precious, life-affirming place. But to understand how it is that Akaya has given me this faith, it's necessary to understand a little more of her own story.

If there was ever somebody for whom the old narrative wasn't intended, it's Akaya Windwood. A queer Black woman born in the United States at the beginning of the Civil Rights Movement, the old story found countless ways —physical, emotional, and mental—to let Akaya know that the privilege of shaping change wasn't hers to be had.

But the story told to her by the outside world was in stark contrast to that being told at home in her inner world. Akaya describes growing up in the 60s, with both parents prominent civil-rights activists with important roles in the local NAACP. With their family living room as a constant gathering place for meetings, she understood early on that taking responsibility for shaping change was a part of who she was.

Navigating the world with these two seemingly irreconcilable stories was challenging and often painful. Hers was a childhood full of moments such as in late 1963 when, just seven years old, she took a seat on the first bus in their town to integrate. Two black kids per white school was the recipe for integration. "There were just eight of us on the bus, which drove around dropping us off two by two by two by two," she explained. "It was the hardest thing I'd ever done. The teacher didn't speak to me, the kids didn't speak to me, no one spoke to me. I felt invisible."

And in many ways, she was. At least to the larger system and dominant powers that resisted this move toward greater justice and equality. She stops her reflection, then looks directly at me. "Not being seen hurts. You know that."

I do. I think about all of the young people who I've worked with for whom the dominant narrative and a single story of poverty or difference rendered them silent and invisible, useful only as statistics or numbers. Two per school.

I remember a comment Loida had made during one of our interviews, that a weaver must learn to see each thread, and reflect back on my first impression of Akaya. Here was an interesting differential. Most of the powerful and influential people I had met in my lifetime had made me feel invisible, inconsequential. But Akaya was the opposite. With her I felt seen, sometimes even uncomfortably so. I wonder out loud if this experience of being invisible is what taught Akaya to see people.

She thinks about it for a few seconds. "Maybe. But I think that has more to do with having to learn how to pay attention. It's a survival strategy. When you're on the margins, you have to learn to pay attention because if you don't, you die."

It is a sombre twist to Loida's own advice to pay attention. Her comment affirms my own belief that the voices on the fringes hold many of the answers to our greatest challenges. As I listen to Akaya talk, I'm reminded that adversity can be a teacher as much as any mentor, if we stay curious about the lessons it is offering us.

I ask Akaya to tell me a little more about the role of adversity in her life, fully expecting her to tell me a story about growing up with the challenges of racism, sexism, classism, and homophobia. But I was wrong.

Instead, Akaya surprises me. "I came of age at a time when everything was possible. Everything. Was. Possible," she emphasizes. For Akaya, the huge freedom she experienced at the time as a young, Black lesbian in the early 70s was fertile ground for the seed that had been planted in her childhood—the idea that anyone could shape change.

This seed was the beginning of a new story, a story that said a queer Black woman in the United States *did* have the power, position, permission, and perspective to shape change. Akaya continued to nourish and nurture that story throughout her 20s and into her early 30s. But what she wasn't aware of was that despite having written this new story, despite an exciting cultural narrative at the time telling her anything was possible, the underlying patterns on which all of this was built were incompatible.

In her early thirties, studying a PhD in clinical psychology at UC Berkeley, she started coming up against barriers she hadn't experienced before. "They were like these invisible walls," says Akaya, "and you don't know they're there unless you hit them."

I nod in understanding. "Glass hurdles" is my name for them, a common experience for those of us that get lulled into believing there might just be a place for us in the old narrative. Until one of those glass hurdles trips us up or we slam into an invisible wall. Akaya began getting tripped up every way she turned. She could find no way forward, and so, with only her dissertation remaining, she walked away.

This was a pivotal moment in Akaya's work as a change maker.

One of the consequences of the individualistic narrative is that it diminishes our ability to see paradigms as distinct from the individuals that live within and are affected by them. In other words, we tend to take them personally.

But not Akaya. "I realized that this wasn't about me. This was about systems (AKA patterns)." In order for her own story to truly flourish, she needed to change the context within which her story was told, the building blocks on which it was built. This realization set her on the path to leadership development, where she spent the greater part of two decades helping thousands of leaders, spanning myriad sectors to learn to be better leaders.

But what is a better leader, exactly? I think back once again to my first impressions of Akaya, that overwhelming sense of power and influence. I try to imagine anyone trying to tell Akaya she didn't have the power, permission, position, or perspective to create change and can't help but smile. "So tell me about power," I say to Akaya.

She thinks for a minute. "My power comes from my relationship to my communities. I am powerful because they request and allow it. The depth and quality of those interrelationships, to be trusted, that is my source of strength and power. I hold myself to high standards to walking in alignment with what I am trying to bring into the world." Then she chuckles. "All of these people who act as though it was a power pie. Power isn't finite. Power is like love—infinite."

Her words speak to me, and I'm reminded of the quote from Buddha about happiness: "Thousands of candles can be lit from a single candle, and the life of the candle will not be shortened. Happiness never decreases by being shared." So it is with love. So it is with power. So it is, I think, with most things Weaver. A world built on abundance, not scarcity where, as Akaya says, my gift complements your gift, and neither is supreme.

The year after I met Akaya, she was named one of Conscious Company's Thirty World-Changing Women. As I reflect on the award itself, I'm mindful of how apt a recognition it is for her. It's not the First 100, Top 500, or Next 1000. There is no comparison or competitive ranking required.

It's a simple but profound statement of Akaya Windwood's ability to shape change. I think back to my image of Akaya moving among the conference delegates. A candle, lighting up other flames, bringing brightness and light. *This* was not *that,* I had thought at the time. No, that's right.

This was a Weaver walking.

THE WEAVER'S WAY
FRAMEWORK SUMMARY

FIVE GUIDING PRINCIPLES

Principle 1: Dance with Tension
Principle 2: Tender Humility
Principle 3: Cultivate Curiosity
Principle 4: Practice Agility and Contextual Responsiveness
Principle 5: Embrace Timefullness

THREE WEAVING LORES

Lore 1: People-driven Partnerships
Lore 2: Process-Centric Approaches
Lore 3: Rooted in Place

SEVEN STRATEGIES FOR EFFECTIVE WEAVING

Strategy 1: How to Prevent Knots
Strategy 2: Choose your Loom
Strategy 3: Don't Overpower, Empower
Strategy 4: Find the Rhythm of the Weave
Strategy 5: Embrace Emergence
Strategy 6: Pay Attention to The Edges
Strategy 7: Attend, Mend, Repair

PART THREE
WEAVER AS LEADER, LEADER AS WEAVER

CHAPTER 11
A TRIBUTE TO THE WEAVERS

> To be hopeful means to be uncertain about the future, to
> be tender toward possibilities, to be dedicated to change
> all the way down to the bottom of your heart.

— REBECCA SOLNIT

When I first started writing this book I was often questioned about whether this was a book about creating change or a book about leadership. In my own head they were synonymous, but I knew there was a lot of wishful thinking that joined the two together: I wished our traditional Leaders would adopt more Weaver qualities, and I wanted the Weavers of the world to be seen as the incredible leaders they were. What a world it would be, I often thought, if we could eliminate the juxtaposition that seems to arise when we place Leaders and Weavers side by side.

Then one day while writing, in one of my frequent research dalliances with the internet, an article popped up on my LinkedIn feed. It was an interview with an acquaintance to whom I had been loosely connected through professional circles for some years, although I had never had the opportunity to learn more about her story. "If it didn't have to be me leading, then it shouldn't be me" was the highlighted quote that grabbed my attention, highly tuned as I was to stories of alternative leadership models. Intrigued, I clicked on the link that would take me down the rabbit hole to learn more about Ayla Schlosser. After speaking with Ayla, I am hopeful, once again, that there is a future, a leaderful future, where Weavers are Leaders, and Leaders are Weavers.

WEAVER: AYLA SCHLOSSER

The first thing that struck me as I read about her work was how similar—at least by outward appearances—Ayla's and my own journey had been. Of a similar age, we'd both been driven by a desire to do change differently that had caused us to journey far from our places of origin, finding roots among people and places very different from our own. Myself from Australia to Guatemala; Ayla from the United States to Rwanda. Without intending to, we'd both started then led organizations in those countries—organizations focused on supporting the leadership of marginalized populations to make changes in their lives and communities. Then we'd purposefully and intentionally stepped aside from those roles to make way for local leaders to run the organizations.

Now here we both were, on the other side of those life-changing experiences. I was eager to compare notes. After reading the article I also had a hunch that here was someone else for whom the idea of Weaver and Leader were not so very different. Perhaps together, Ayla could help me to make the connection between the two a little less ephemeral, a little more tangible.

The Weaver way of thinking about leading and leadership is a defining characteristic of Resonate, the organization Ayla helped to co-found in Rwanda in 2013 and which has now trained over 12,000 women and girls across East Africa. The starting point for the organization is a firm conviction that leadership isn't about a role or a title but a way of being. A way of being, explained Ayla, "that is proactive in the face of a challenge." It's a simple and inclusive definition that invites Resonate's participants— regardless of their background—to begin to see their potential for creating change in the world around them.

Resonate's approach is to get participants to consider two fundamental questions: "How do you see yourself?" and "How do you relate to the world?" Here once again is the complementary work of being and doing, innervism and activism, The Weaver and Weaving. As Ayla explained it, "Just by changing those two things, you can change the world around you."

Resonate's work helps participants to see that just by taking leadership in their own lives, they can begin to have a positive impact on the world around them. "Because we are connected," said Ayla, "the leadership of the women and girls we work with creates impacts on their families and communities, which then have a broader impact on culture."

This is how they help women and girls develop the confidence to take action and create change. As Ayla and many of the others I interviewed for this book affirm, this small shift is a powerful leverage point for creating wider change, by setting up a positive feedback loop that encourages the person to continue to widen their sphere of impact. "By this measure, anyone can be a leader. It's not that it's easy or simple," remarked Ayla, "but it is possible."

Another element that's integral in Resonate's approach is their use of storytelling to shape change. The powerful and transformative role of storytelling was something Ayla discovered early on in her own journey while working as a community organizer in Washington, DC. Like many of us, as a young person Ayla had unquestioningly absorbed the narratives handed her from community and society about what it meant to be good and successful, but that had led to a compromising situation and a difficult time in Ayla's life.

Then one day at a public narrative workshop for community organizers, Ayla was invited to examine her own stories. "I was suddenly confronted by the story of what I told about myself," she recalls, "and I was shocked. I suddenly realized that all of my stories were about other things and other people. I knew how to advocate, but not to self-advocate." This realization was an important pivot point in Ayla's journey. She saw how the act of claiming ownership of our stories and giving voice to them was a powerful way to free people from the pain of the past and engage them in taking action for the future.

"If we build on this idea that leadership is partly how you relate to yourself and partly how you relate to the world," explained Ayla, "then voice is how we bridge that gap, and stories are how we express our voice. Over and over again, I watched the people I was working with step into the power of their own voice, simply by asking the question 'What story are you telling about yourself, and how can we make that a story of your own choosing?' It was transformative."

In this process, she also saw how storytelling could be a powerful tool for recruiting agency, which is what eventually drew her to Rwanda. It was a time when smart economics and women's economic empowerment were gaining traction, and there was a huge wave of investing in women, particularly in international development. But Ayla was concerned about what appeared to be an excessive focus on new products and programs. "So many women in these settings are already overburdened with so many other responsibilities, the last thing they needed was to be given a six-month training, or complicated income-generating activity or multi-step framework to follow. I just kept wondering, what if we just helped give them access to themselves and their own voice?"

It's an approach that seems to be working. A randomized control trial[1] (RCT) conducted by researchers at UC Berkeley and Georgetown University found that those who went through Resonate's three-day leadership workshops were sixty-seven percent more likely to speak up in a public setting, thirty-four percent more likely to identify as a leader, thirty-one percent more likely to achieve their goals, and earned 116 percent more income than those who didn't go through the training. It's more proof of the transformative impact of Weaver approaches.

But Ayla is the first to admit Resonate's success wasn't because of some well-planned project idea. In fact, she admits it's precisely because she didn't know what she was doing, which made her approach the work with a deep sense of curiosity and humility. "It's much more valuable to be curious than to be an expert. Besides, you can't be an expert in a place you aren't from. You have to understand that what you have to offer is valuable only in so much as you first understand how it's useful."

Ayla knew she had to discover the knowledge and wisdom in the place she was working. "Many things were missing, but I knew how to ask questions and how to listen. As a result, the women we were working with were at the centre of everything we did." In Resonate's work, it's easy to see the people, process, place-based approach of *The Weaver's Way* and how this leads to impact. As Ayla writes, "We've seen the incredible changes that take place when we trust the women we work with to take charge of their lives and create the changes they want to see in their lives and communities."

No longer at the helm of Resonate, I asked Ayla what she has learned from the women she worked with and how we might use that wisdom to tackle some of the big, seemingly intractable problems we face today. Ayla told me that when it comes to shaping change, whether it's change in your local neighborhood or some of the complex problems she is now supporting, by advising local leaders working to combat problems like climate change and child sexual abuse, she believes that the scariest, most intimidating moment is right before you begin. "Before I become immersed in the problems, they seem unwinnable. But the second I take the step, I become more hopeful. Because all around me, I discover a flurry of people taking steps."

All around, we are surrounded by Weavers.

I HOPE THAT HEARING THE STORIES OF AYLA, AKAYA, RICHIE, TOPHER, PATTY, Haile, Therese, and Joyce has inspired you and invited you to dream of new possibilities. Perhaps you've identified old stories or narratives that you need to replace to build something new. Perhaps it has caused you to look around and find ways you can leverage your privileges to lift up and shine a light on someone else's efforts. Or maybe you've begun to think about your own identities and experiences and how those diverse lenses could shape the way you approach your work.

They certainly did for me.

While I was familiar with the work of the people we've met in the Weaver's Guild, I'd never had the opportunity to hear their stories in such depth, and it was a wonderful and humbling experience. It was affirming to see the guiding principles constantly at work. It was encouraging to hear how the Weaver's Lores had been used to change the lives of so many people and places.

In a final review of my notes from our conversations, I also noticed there were three other elements that seemed to be universal to all of their stories, which I believe are insightful when it comes to thinking about our own roles as Weavers.

The first thing I noticed was that for each person, the aspects of *The Weaver's Way* framework that were showcased with their story invariably turned out to be different from what I'd originally contemplated. The elements I'd thought to highlight were still there, but as I listened I found there were other aspects that seemed to be more appropriate to the telling of their story.

As I reflected on this, I realized that it's a consequence to be expected in the holistic framework of *The Weaver's Way* and the non-linear process of Weaving. It's as difficult to point to someone's story and say "this is an example of such-and-such guiding principle" as it is to look at a finished tapestry and pinpoint the contribution only of the magenta thread. The guiding principles and Lores are interconnected, complementary, and mutually reinforcing. You will see this for yourself as you begin to put them into practice.

The second thing I noticed during the interviews was that for these Weavers, Weaving wasn't a job. It's true that for some, much of their work was in the formal change sector. But the Weaver way of doing and being showed up in many different aspects of their lives. Yes, there were ample examples of Weaving in their work. But The Weaver's Way also showed up in how they parented, how they engaged with their wider community, and how they related to themselves.

It was, truly, a way of working and walking in the world.

No matter how much they'd accomplished, I also realized none of the people I interviewed would look at their work and consider it finished. They would all consider both themselves and their efforts as "a work in progress"—an acknowledgement that they are all very much still on their Weaver journeys. The work continues, and so do they.

The final aspect that emerged in speaking with all of the people I interviewed—and something that's true of my own experience—is joy. Being a Weaver is not about being a martyr. Even though the work of Weaving often asks us to be closer to pain and suffering, that very opening is a doorway to joy itself. Perhaps it's because we find a greater sense of purpose. Perhaps it's the joy of being in relationships with people who see you as your true self. Or perhaps, as Akaya notes, it's because our souls are Weavers, that have been waiting to be set free. And that in that freedom comes the discovery of a new world.

A world wherein Wilbur and his peers are leaders, capable of fighting injustice and bringing about change. A world where indigenous Guatemalan women are examples of strength, resilience and resistance against the hegemonic forces of colonization and free market capitalism. A world that celebrates the courage, bravery, and leadership of people like Billy.

CAPTAIN BILLY AND THE TIN BOAT

All throughout the day, the rain continued to fall. The realization would come to me all of a sudden—while carrying fuel to a waiting boat or reaching out to take a baby from her mother's arms. "It's still coming," I'd mutter incredulously to no one in particular. Wiping the water out of my eyes, I'd glance up at the heavy gray sky. "Let it stop," I begged. A silent, desperate plea to the heavens above. "Can't you see how hard we're trying?"

Apparently, neither God nor Mother Nature subscribe to the meritocracy myth, either. Effort has nothing to do with it.

As I moved from one need to the next, I kept thinking of the people still over on the south side of town. Since that first early-morning rescue when the boat I was on had been damaged, I hadn't been able to find anyone else willing to make the treacherous crossing. I asked every boat driver I came across but received the same response each time—a shaking of the head, a regretful shrugging of the shoulders. The river's too strong. The waters are too dangerous. A boat this size won't make it. There's plenty to do here.

And it was true. For hours we had been going nonstop. But still. On the south side there *was* no higher ground. That, and I'd promised I'd go back.

I picked up a couple of bananas off the ground from where someone had considerately thought to leave a pile of snacks for the impromptu rescuers and their passengers. Peeling one, I carried the other over to where an older man had a boat pulled up in the front yard of a house that I had been watching slowly succumb to the water all morning. "Got it going yet?" I asked by way of greeting, the banana proffered in front of me in lieu of a handshake. He looked up at me. He appeared to be of Southeast Asian descent with sparse gray hair, a short gray beard, and large black glasses sitting crookedly across the end of his nose.

"I reckon we're good to go," he declared, giving me a smile that was more gums than teeth. "Are you coming?"

I jumped in. "Get as far up the front as you can," he yelled as we started out. "Hang over the bow if possible—we don't know what's in the water."

"Got it," I responded, turning back to look at him as I climbed up onto the triangular prow of the small tin boat.

"What's your name?"

"Billy."

Billy and I ran a couple of trips, each one getting a little harder to get back as the water continued to add new obstacles. After the third or fourth trip back, as we unloaded a young Sudanese family—grim-faced adults and exuberant young boys happily ensconced in the blissful ignorance of childhood and the thrill of their first boat ride—Billy turned to me. "I think this area's pretty well covered," he remarked. I looked around. He was right. By now there were plenty of boats and support people, all working together to move people from high point to high point across the flooded town and up into the evacuation centers. Emergent strategy at its best. While there was still ample need, the abrasive, urgent edge of the morning seemed to have dissipated.

"Now what?" he asked me. I bit my lip, looked at Billy, and paused to take a deep breath. It was worth one more try.

"What about the South side? The crossing's hard, it's dangerous, I don't know if this boat will make it..." It all came out in a rush. I stopped and took another breath. "But no one seems willing to go there, and there are heaps of people—families—who need help." Even as I said it, I wondered how much I really understood what I was signing us both up for.

When discussing some of the questionable scenarios I've gotten myself into over my lifetime, I often joke that it isn't that I'm fearless, it's that I have an under-developed amygdala (that is pure speculation, not a medical diagnosis by the way). I wondered if this was another of those situations.

Billy, however, was unfazed. "All right. Tell me where you want to go, and I'll take you there."

I felt it then. That moment when the seeking tendrils of trust find something solid to grasp onto and suddenly *me* becomes *we*. Significant, despite its brevity.

I looked at Billy. Took in his bare feet. His sodden red track pants and fluorescent yellow traffic worker's rain jacket. His thick glasses, so fogged up I had no idea how he'd been able to navigate at all. The deep, weathered lines on his face. "All right, Captain Billy." I nodded. "Let's do it."

Getting to the south side felt like switching the channels on the television from the British Antiques Roadshow into the climax of a Hollywood war movie. I leaned over the bow, yelling back warnings:

dead horse, gas cylinder, shipping container, the top of the overhead railway bridge. The smell of gasoline washed over us as we passed over where a gas station used to be, and I tried not to imagine what would happen if something threw out a spark.

We navigated to the main intersection on the south side of town, near the railway station. All was chaos. The two rivers seemed to have decided that this intersection would work well for them as well, and the coming together of these two fast flowing bodies of water threw up large, irregular waves. On the corner of the intersection, twenty or thirty people crowded onto the verandah of the old railway hotel. Boats and Jet Skis moved back and forth carrying people and animals.

As we made our way across the intersection a wave lifted us up, bringing us down with a thud. Suddenly we were stuck, broadside to the raging torrent.

"What's happening?" yelled Billy.

"We're caught on the roof of the railway station." I called back. Even I, with little knowledge of boats, knew we were at risk of capsizing with the boat broadside of the current. "Get all of your weight over this side," Billy urged.

A man on a Jet Ski saw us and came over. "Throw me a line and I'll pull you off," he called out. As he began trying to drag us off the roof, I looked back at Billy, who was staring upstream at the maelstrom of boats, Jet Skis, and raging flood water. As I followed the direction of his gaze, a Jet Ski and boat suddenly collided, throwing the Jet Ski's two passengers into the river. As though he'd seen it coming, Billy turned immediately to our rescuer. "Leave us," yelled Billy. "Go, go, go." The Jet Ski tore off, chasing down a man whose head was underwater, his cat held high as the river rushed them away. Another wave washed us up, and Billy immediately gunned the engine. We were away.

"This area's covered," said Billy. "Let's keep going." I nodded in agreement. But we hadn't gone more than a few hundred meters when another wave lifted us up, this time bringing us down with a tearing sound and an abrupt jerk as we stopped still, the engine revving uselessly. I looked down into the center of the boat: we were impaled, a four-inch post going straight through the bottom of the boat.

By this point, even my amygdala was starting to pay attention. I looked helplessly at Billy. "There's a pole through the boat! We're stuck." He left the motor and came to look. "Grab that towel," he said, indicating a towel he'd handed me earlier in the day, in an attempt to stop my uncontrollable shivering. I passed him the towel.

"Okay. When we come off the post, shove the towel in the hole. Then stand on it, with all of your weight."

Holy shit, I thought to myself. As I contemplated how betrayed I felt by this floating tin can, Billy called out to a passing boat. "Can you pull us off?" The boat's driver grabbed the line.

"Ready?" said Billy. Again, I nodded. Our boat, free once again and our makeshift plug in place, Billy passed me a bucket. "Do you know how to bail?"

I laughed once. "Like my life depends on it," I told him, as I furiously started scooping out bucketfuls of water.

Billy revved up the engine once again and pointed us back up the street-cum-river. "Are you okay?" he asked.

"Yeah, I'm good."

"All right," he said. "Where to next?"

DESTINATION: A MORE BEAUTIFUL WORLD

It is at times like that day out rescuing flood victims that I think back to the beginning of my own unexpected journey, many years ago. That first trip to Guatemala, feeling so alone and heartbroken, convinced that my world had ended.

In a way, I guess it had. It was the end of a world of myth and fantasy. Of old narratives, and stories written for another time. But it was also the beginning of a new world, a new reality.

I may not have as much money as I did back in my old world, with my high-flying corporate career. But I am infinitely wealthier.

I may not be loved by the one whom I once considered the love of my life. But I am loved much more authentically and deeply than I ever dreamed possible.

I may not have found "the one," as a woman of my age is expected to have done. But I revel in the fact that I am not loved by one, but by many. A community of people, the breadth, depth, and diversity of which takes my breath away.

I may not be considered as powerful as when I dressed in a power suit and rode the elevator to the top of the tallest office building, but the power that I do hold is more meaningful and purposeful. It's a power that is regenerative, not extractive, and that holds me accountable to living a life aligned with my values and beliefs.

I ran into Billy a few weeks after that first flood hit Lismore. I was out with my sister, taking hot coffee and cake to people who were doing the exhausting work of trying to clean their flood-ravaged houses. As we drove past a lookout above town, I glanced out the window, remembering how just a few weeks ago it had been nothing but a sea of brown. As I did, I noticed a man sitting at one of the picnic tables, playing a guitar.

"Stop the car," I said to my sister. "I think that's Billy." We parked and I jumped out. "Captain Billy!" I shouted joyfully. He looked up, smiling that wonderful, gap-toothed smile. "I thought you might like some cake," I said, mirroring with my own toothy grin. "And I want to introduce you to my sister."

My sister came up and immediately gave Billy a huge hug. "Thank you for helping all of those people," she said. "Thank you for keeping my sister safe." He pulled away from my sister.

"It's so great to see you," I said, going in for my own hug. "I thought you had to go away for work?"

He looked at us both and his eyes filled with tears. "No." He shook his head adamantly. "How could I? This is *my* town. These are *my* people. There's work to be done right here."

No, I'll never be a princess living a life of luxury in my tower within a walled city. Thank goodness. I see only loss and loneliness in that world of separation and isolation. And I've realized that I'll never find a shiny knight on his white horse. I don't need to. Because I've got people like Captain Billy and his tin boat. "Where to next?" Billy had asked me.

I know where I'm heading. To borrow a phrase from economist and author Charles Eisenstein, I'm headed to the more beautiful world that our hearts know is possible.

CHAPTER 12
THE POWER OF PERSPECTIVE

J ames Suzman, an anthropologist who has studied the history of
humankind through the prism of work, explains that it was the
agricultural revolution that began the trend in which *what* we
did and *where* we did it—as in our work—defined much of our
identity.[1] We became the Coopers, the Smiths, the Canners and
created a legacy that we carry with us today. Not just in our surnames
but in the stories we share. We meet someone new, and our first
question invariably is, "What do you do?"

But what if this next stage of the human story was defined not by
what we do but by why and how? Tell me a story of how you're
working to shape change, you would ask. And I would tell you a story
of meaning and hope and joy. Where once we were the Coopers, the
Smiths, and the Canners in this new story, we could become The
Weavers.

I believe we are at a decisive moment in human history. A moment
in which we must acknowledge that the challenges we face cannot be
solved by any one individual, organization, or government alone. It
requires us all. Our old stories convinced us we did not have the power,
permission, position, or perspective to shape change. Our new story

gives us the privilege to do so. As social scientist Shankar Vedantam writes in his book, *Useful Delusions: The Power and Paradox of the Self-Deceiving Brain,* if we believe a story to be true, then that story has real power.[2] So which story do we choose to believe?

It's time to seize authorship over the unwritten future. We have a choice whether to perpetuate the stories of old or to change them. As Rebecca Solnit writes, "Stories surround us like air; we breathe them in, we breathe them out. The art of being fully conscious in personal life means seeing the stories and becoming their teller, rather than letting them be the unseen forces that tell you what to do."[3]

Every story you tell that illuminates a new way of working contributes to the collection. Every question you ask with an inquiring mind, encouraging curiosity, and insight, belongs. Every time you purposefully engage in shaping change toward a better future builds hope. Start where you are, use what you have, do what you can.

I began writing *The Weaver's Way* hoping to inspire you to join me in shaping change for a more just and equitable future for people and our planet. But what is hope in the face of so much uncertainty?

In Part I, I talked about the powerful transformation that was possible when we began to help marginalized and vulnerable youth to change their story. In changing their story, we didn't remove the uncertainty. The outcome still is, and always will be, uncertain. But we gave them hope. Hope for a safer home. Hope for a better future. And hope that they, themselves, could play a role in building that future.

When I was interviewing Therese Caouette, she reminded me of the powerful role that hope plays in the life of a Weaver. After we finished our call, she sent through an email with this poignant quote from Václav Havel, the last president of Czechoslovakia and the first President of the Czech Republic. Havel writes:

> Hope is a state of mind, not of the world. Either we have hope within us or we don't; it is a dimension of the soul, and it's not essentially dependent on some particular observation of the world or estimate of the situation.

Hope is not prognostication. It is an orientation of the spirit, an orientation of the heart; it transcends the world that is immediately experienced and is anchored somewhere beyond its horizons. Hope, in this deep and powerful sense, is not the same as joy that things are going well, or willingness to invest in enterprises that are obviously heading for success, but rather the ability to work for something because it is good, not just because it stands a chance to succeed. The more preposterous the situation in which we demonstrate hope, the deeper the hope is. Hope is definitely not the same thing as optimism. It is not the conviction that something will turn out well, but the certainty that something makes sense, regardless of how it turns out.[4]

We are at a *kairos* moment in human history—an opportune moment—and the decisions and actions we make now will be instrumental in shaping the future. All people everywhere must realize their leadership potential, working to shape systems and move beyond business as usual approaches. We need strong partnerships and collective actions that bridge across traditional boundaries and transcend polarizing discussions, collaborations that leverage our inner capacities and leadership skills to create, build, and heal.

Let's take off our masks of difference and indifference and commit ourselves to creating the world to which we aspire. As civil-rights activist Valarie Kaur writes: "When a critical mass of people come together to wonder about one another, grieve with one another, and fight with and for one another, we begin to build the solidarity needed for collective liberation and transformation—a solidarity rooted in love."[5]

With every step we take along this path of unity, collaboration, and service, we move closer to that more beautiful world: a just and equitable future for all people and our planet.

CHANGE IS IN YOUR HANDS

A close friend of mine, Elena (not her real name), was going through a hard time. She was a mother with two young kids in school, working part time. She's the kind of person who gave everything of herself to those she loved—her kids, her family, her work—which didn't leave much for herself. In fact, the one area that she lacked discipline was around self-care, and that was starting to take its toll on her health and well-being.

It was about this time that there was a crisis at the school her children attended. The president of the parent-teacher committee was stepping down, leaving not only her role but all officer positions vacant. No one was willing to step up, but without volunteers there would be no committee, and ultimately it would be the kids who would be impacted.

Elena is not the kind of person who can see a need without trying to do something about it. And so despite running on empty, she stepped up and said yes to getting the committee up and going again. But even as she said yes, she was angry and resentful. She felt as though she had no choice and had been left alone and abandoned by the other parents. I watched her with growing concern as this additional burden she had agreed to carry took its emotional and physical toll.

Throughout *The Weaver's Way* I have talked about the idea that the work of shaping change should be joyful. I mean this in the strongest possible sense. Because when it isn't joyful—irrespective of our dedication and commitment—we are simply unable to bring our best selves. The resulting emotional energy is draining on both ourselves and those around us. And one of the keys to finding this joy is choice. When we feel we have the agency to choose where we want to shape change, it can be a true source of joy and inspiration.

Toward the end of that year walking along the beach with my friend, she shared with me that she was thinking of resigning from her role as president on the committee once the term was up. "I want to resign, but I can't get over the feeling that I'm a failure for quitting and didn't get done everything I wanted to do."

"It sounds to me like you've made some amazing changes," I observed. "You built up the committee, got more people interested in being a part of it, and started some great initiatives. It also doesn't have to be a forever decision. Take the time you need for you. You can come back when you're feeling you've got more space for it."

I also shared—cautiously—my belief that we should never engage with change purely out of a sense of obligation. It just breeds resentment, which isn't good for anyone involved. "You've done a great job. Now take some time for yourself."

A few weeks later, catching up over the phone, I asked if she'd shared with the other committee members her decision not to run again.

"Actually," she said, "I think I will."

"Wow," I responded, more than a little surprised. Not at the decision, but at the lighthearted way she shared the news, such a difference to what I'd been hearing all year. "So what changed?"

"My perspective," she said. "That conversation on the beach helped me shift from seeing this as something I was forced to do, and feeling alone and angry because of that, to something I was choosing to step into, bringing my gifts and abilities with me to do a great job. When I realized I had a choice, everything changed."

The take-away? It was the same set of circumstances, but a completely different outcome!

I just love this story because I think there are a number of beautiful Weaver gems here. It shows how powerful perspective can be and that the power to change that perspective is in our own hands. It emphasizes how important it is to practice agility so that we can become more skilled at being able to make those changes in perspective. And it reminds me how important agency is, that *all* of us feel we have choice in shaping the world around us.

BIBLIOGRAPHY

Adichie, Chimamanda, 2016. "The Danger of a Single Story." https://www.ted.com/talks/chimamanda_adichie_the_danger_of_a_single_story/transcript?language=en, Accessed 10 March 2022.

AI Commons. "Introduction to Appreciative Inquiry." Accessed July 8, 2022. https://appreciativeinquiry.champlain.edu/learn/appreciative-inquiry-introduction/

Arablouei, Ramtin, and Abdelfatah Rund. *"Throughline."* Podcast audio. NPR.

Barghouti, Mourid, Ahdaf Soueif, and Mourid Barghouti. 2005. *I Saw Ramallah*. London: Bloomsbury.

Baldwin, James. "As Much Truth As One Can Bear." *The New York Times Book Review*. January 14, 1962.

Boggs, Grace Lee. Quoted in Bonfiglio, Olga. "You Say You Want a Revolution?" [online]. Common Dreams. July 20, 2008. https://www.commondreams.org/views/2008/07/20/you-say-you-want-revolution Accessed on June 4, 2021.

Brafman, Ori, and Rod A. Beckstrom. 2014. *The Starfish and the Spider: The Unstoppable Power of Leaderless Organizations*. New York: Portfolio.

Brown, Adrienne M. 2017. *Emergent Strategy*. Chico, CA: AK Press.

Brown, Brené. 2018. *Dare to Lead: Brave Work, Tough Conversations, Whole Hearts*. London: Vermilion.

Brown, Brené. 2015. "Own Our History. Change The Story." www.brenebrown.com (blog). June 18, 2015. https://brenebrown.com/articles/2015/06/18/own-our-history-change-the-story/ .

Butler, Octavia E. 2000. *Parable of the Sower*. Warner Books ed. New York: Warner Books.

Community Canvas. "Community Canvas." Accessed June 28, 2022. https://community-canvas.org/ .

Denham, Amanda. 2017. "The Predicament of Maya Textiles in the South Highlands of Guatemala: What is Authenticity and Where Can I Buy It?" (master's thesis, Cornell University), https://doi.org/10.7298/X4V9867S .

Eisenstein, Charles. 2021. *Sacred Economics: Money, Gift and Society in the Age of Transition*. Revised edition. Berkeley, California: North Atlantic Books.

Galeano, Eduardo. "Interview with Eduardo Galeano." By David Barsamian. *The Progressive* 63, no. 7 (July 1999): 35-38.

Giridharadas, Anand. 2020. *Winners Take All: The Elite Charade of Changing the World*. London: Penguin Books.

Gladwell, Malcom. "My Little Hundred Million," September 25, 2017, in *Revisionist History*, produced by Pushkin Industries, podcast audio, https://www.pushkin.fm/podcasts/revisionist-history/my-little-hundred-million .

Gladwell, Malcolm. 2019. *Talking to Strangers: What We Should Know about the People We Don't Know*. New York: Little, Brown and Company.

Grant, Adam M. 2018. *Power Moves: Lessons from Davos*. Audible. Audiobook.

Grant, Adam M. 2021. *Think Again: The Power of Knowing What You Don't Know*. New York, New York: Viking.

Grant, Adam, and Sheryl Sandberg. 2017. *Originals: How Non-Conformists Move the World*. New York, New York: Viking.

Havel, Vaclav. Quoted in Yates, Richard. 1975. *Disturbing the Peace*. New York: Delacorte Press/S. Lawrence.

Kaur, Valarie. 2020. *See No Stranger: A Memoir and Manifesto of Revolutionary Love*. First edition. New York: One World.

Laloux, Frédéric, and Ken Wilber. 2014. *Reinventing Organizations: A Guide to Creating Organizations Inspired by the Next Stage of Human Consciousness*. First edition. Brussels: Nelson Parker.

Liberating Structures: Including and Unleashing Everyone. Accessed January 14, 2022. http://www.liberatingstructures.com/.

Lorde, Audre. 2018. *The Master's Tools Will Never Dismantle the Master's House*. Penguin Modern. London, England: Penguin Classics.

Maalouf, Amin. 2012. *In the Name of Identity: Violence and the Need to Belong*. Translated by Barbara Bray. New York: Arcade Publishing.

Macy, Joanna, and Molly Young Brown. 2014. *Coming Back to Life: The Updated Guide to the Work That Reconnects*. Gabriola Island, British Columbia, Canada: New Society Publishers.

Martin, Roger. n.d. "What Is Integrative Thinking?" I-Think. Accessed May 15, 2021. https://www.i-thinktogether.org/what-is-integrative-thinking.

Mazzucato, Mariana. 2018. *The Value of Everything: Making and Taking in the Global Economy*. [London], UK: Allen Lane, an imprint of Penguin Books.

Merrill, Susan Barrett. 2016. *The Art of Weaving a Life: A Framework to Expand and Strengthen Your Personal Vision*. Atglen, PA: Schiffer Publishing, Ltd.

Moreton-Robinson, Aileen. *Talkin' up to the White Woman: Indigenous Women and Feminism*. St Lucia: UQP, 2000.

Nicholas, Chani. 2021. "New Moon in Libra: Horoscopes for the Week of September 26th." Chani. September 26, 2021. https://chaninicholas.com/.

Nepo, Mark. 2012. *Seven Thousand Ways to Listen: Staying Close to What Is Sacred*. New York: Free Press.

Parker, Priya. 2018. *The Art of Gathering: Create Transformative Meetings, Events and Experiences*.

Peavey, Fran. *Strategic Questioning Manual: A Powerful Tool for Personal and Social Change*. The Commons. *https://commonslibrary.org/strategic-questioning/*.

Pope Francis, 2017. "Why the Only Future Worth Building Includes Everyone." [online] Ted.com. https://www.ted.com/talks/his_holiness_pope_francis_why_the_only_future_worth_building_includes_everyone?language=en. Accessed 13 November 2021.

Niebuhr, Reinhold. 2013. *Moral Man and Immoral Society: A Study in Ethics and Politics*. Second edition. Library of Theological Ethics. Louisville, KY: Westminster John Knox Press.

Raworth, Kate. 2018. *Doughnut Economics: Seven Ways to Think like a 21st-Century Economist.* Paperback edition. London: Random House Business Books.

Rilke, Rainer Maria, Franz Xaver Kappus, and Stephen Mitchell. 1987. *Letters to a Young Poet.* 1st Vintage Books ed. New York: Vintage Books.

Roy, Arundhati. 2019. *My Seditious Heart: Collected Nonfiction.* Chicago: Haymarket Books.

Scharmer, C. Otto. 2012. *Theory u.* Readhowyouwant.com Ltd.

Schumacher, E. F., and Bill McKibben. 2010. *Small Is Beautiful: Economics as If People Mattered.* First Harper Perennial edition. New York, N.Y: Harper Perennial.

Solnit, Rebecca. 2016. *Hope in the Dark: Untold Histories, Wild Possibilities.* Third edition. Chicago, Illinois: Haymarket Books.

Solnit, Rebecca. 2018. *Call Them by Their True Names: American Crises (and Essays).* Chicago, Illinois: Haymarket Books.

Solnit, Rebecca. 2012. "We Could Be Heroes: An Election-Year Letter." *The Guardian,* October 15, 2012, sec. Guardian Comment Network.

Stevenson, Bryan. *"4 Ways to Fight Injustice"* (Aspen Keynote, Resnick Aspen Action Forum, Aspen, July 19, 2016).

Suzman, James. 2021. *Work: A Deep History, from the Stone Age to the Age of Robots.* New York: Penguin Press.

Toffler, Alvin. 1990. *Future Shock.* New York: Bantam Books.

Tutu, Desmond, South Africa, and Truth and Reconciliation Commission. 1999. *No Future without Forgiveness.* New York: Image.

UNICEF. 2017. "Soy Indígena y También Soy Guatemala." Cuidad de Guatemala: UNICEF. https://www.unicef.org/guatemala/historias/m%C3%ADrame-soy-ind%C3%ADgena-y-tambi%C3%A9n-soy-guatemala.

Vedantum, Shankar, and Bill Mesler. 2022. *Useful Delusions: The Power and Paradox of the Self-Deceiving Brain.* New York: W. W. Norton.

Villanueva, Edgar. 2018. *Decolonizing Wealth: Indigenous Wisdom to Heal Divides and Restore Balance.*

Walker, Darren. 2019. *From Generosity to Justice: A New Gospel of Wealth.* The Ford Foundation/Disruption Books. Available online at: https://www.fordfoundation.org/new-gospel-media/GenerositytoJustice.pdf .

Wheatley, Margaret J. 2017. *Who Do We Choose to Be? Facing Reality, Claiming Leadership, Restoring Sanity.* First edition. Oakland, CA: Berrett-Koehler Publishers Inc.

Wheatley, Margaret J, and Deborah Frieze. 2011. *Walk out Walk on: A Learning Journey into Communities Daring to Live the Future Now.* San Francisco, CA: Berrett-Koehler Publishers Inc.

Notes

INTRODUCTION

1. Roy, Arundhati. 2019. *My Seditious Heart: Collected Nonfiction.* Page 204. Chicago: Haymarket Books.

1. NOT JUST ANOTHER STORY

1. UNICEF. 2017. "Soy Indígena y También Soy Guatemala." Cuidad de Guatemala: UNICEF. https://www.unicef.org/guatemala/historias/m%C3%ADrame-soy-ind%C3%ADgena-y-tambi%C3%A9n-soy-guatemala.
2. Barghouti, Mourid, Ahdaf Soueif, and Mourid Barghouti. 2005. *I Saw Ramallah.* London: Bloomsbury.

2. THE GAMES WE PLAY

1. To build on the idea of the Gift Economy one of my early editors, Professor Michael Gordon, offered the idea of the Gift Ecology, which acknowledges the role of interconnected giving. It's a great evolution of the Gift Economy idea. Thanks, Michael.
2. Adichie, Chimamanda, 2016. "The Danger of a Single Story." [online] Ted.com. https://www.ted.com/talks/chimamanda_adichie_the_danger_of_a_single_story/transcript?language=en, Accessed 10 March 2022.
3. Solnit, Rebecca. 2018. *Call Them by Their True Names: American Crises (and Essays).* Chicago, Illinois: Haymarket Books.
4. HINT: It's known as a "Teal" organization. To read more, have a look at *Reinventing Organizations.*

3. CALLING FORTH THE FUTURE

1. Adichie, Chimamanda, 2016. "The Danger of a Single Story." [online] Ted.com. https://www.ted.com/talks/chimamanda_adichie_the_danger_of_a_single_story/transcript?language=en, Accessed 10 March 2022.

4. A WEAVING METAPHOR

1. Toffler, Alvin. 1990. *Future Shock*. Bantam Books. New York: Bantam Books.
2. Grant, Adam M. 2021. *Think Again: The Power of Knowing What You Don't Know*. New York, New York: Viking.

5. THE WEAVER'S WAY

1. Martin, Roger. n.d. "What Is Integrative Thinking?" I-Think. Accessed May 15, 2021. https://www.i-thinktogether.org/what-is-integrative-thinking.
2. Maalouf, Amin. 2012. *In the Name of Identity: Violence and the Need to Belong*. Translated by Barbara Bray. New York: Arcade Publishing.

6. THE LAWS OF INTERCONNECTEDNESS

1. Moreton-Robinson, Aileen. 2021. *Talkin' Up to the White Woman: Indigenous Women and Feminism*. First University of Minnesota Press edition. Indigenous Americas. Minneapolis: University of Minnesota Press.
2. Tutu, Desmond, South Africa, and Truth and Reconciliation Commission. 1999. *No Future without Forgiveness*. New York: Image.
3. Tutu, Desmond, South Africa, and Truth and Reconciliation Commission. 1999. *No Future without Forgiveness*. New York: Image.
4. Pope Francis, 2017. Transcript of "Why the Only Future Worth Building Includes Everyone." [online] Ted.com. Available at: <https://www.ted.com/talks/his_holiness_pope_francis_why_the_only_future_worth_building_includes_everyone?language=en> [Accessed 13 November 2021].
5. Niebuhr, Reinhold. 2013. *Moral Man and Immoral Society: A Study in Ethics and Politics*. Second edition. Library of Theological Ethics. Louisville, KY: Westminster John Knox Press.
6. Galeano, Eduardo. I"nterview with Eduardo Galeano." By David Barsamian. *The Progressive* 63, no. 7 (July 1999): 35-38.
7. Pope Francis, 2017. Transcript of "Why the Only Future Worth Building Includes Everyone." [online] Ted.com. Available at: <https://www.ted.com/talks/his_holiness_pope_francis_why_the_only_future_worth_building_includes_everyone?language=en> [Accessed 13 November 2021].

7. THE JOURNEY OF BECOMING

1. Stevenson, Bryan. "4 Ways to Fight Injustice." (Aspen Keynote, Resnick Aspen Action Forum, Aspen, July 19, 2016).
2. Brown, Brené. 2018. *Dare to Lead: Brave Work, Tough Conversations, Whole Hearts*. London: Vermilion.

3. Walker, Darren. 2019 *From Generosity to Justice: A New Gospel of Wealth*. The Ford Foundation/Disruption Books. Available online at: https://www.fordfoundation.org/new-gospel-media/GenerositytoJustice.pdf .

8. WEAVING FOR CHANGE

1. Denham, Amanda. 2017. "The Predicament of Maya Textiles in the South Highlands of Guatemala: What is Authenticity and Where Can I Buy It?" (master's thesis, Cornell University), https://doi.org/10.7298/X4V9867S.
2. Grant, Adam M. 2018. *Power Moves: Lessons from Davos*. Audible. Audiobook.
3. Meadows, Donella H., and Club of Rome, eds. 1972. *The Limits to Growth: A Report for the Club of Rome's Project on the Predicament of Mankind*. New York: Universe Books.

9. FINCA ULEW: PLACE OF FIRE

1. Solnit, Rebecca. 2016. *Hope in the Dark: Untold Histories, Wild Possibilities*. Third edition. Chicago, Illinois: Haymarket Books.

10. SEVEN STRATEGIES FOR EFFECTIVE WEAVING

1. Grant, Adam, and Sheryl Sandberg. 2017. *Originals: How Non-Conformists Move the World*. New York, New York: Viking.
2. Lorde, Audre. 2018. *The Master's Tools Will Never Dismantle the Master's House*. Penguin Modern. London, England: Penguin Classics.
3. Gladwell, Malcom. "My Little Hundred Million," September 25, 2017, in *Revisionist History*, produced by Pushkin Industries, podcast audio, https://www.pushkin.fm/podcasts/revisionist-history/my-little-hundred-million .

11. A TRIBUTE TO THE WEAVERS

1. This is considered the gold standard of evaluation for development projects, but because of the cost and scale required to run RCT's, many of the localized, smaller-scale Weaver approaches are not able to run these types of evaluations

12. THE POWER OF PERSPECTIVE

1. Suzman, James. 2021. *Work: A Deep History, from the Stone Age to the Age of Robots*. New York: Penguin Press.
2. Vedantum, Shankar. 2022. *Useful Delusions: The Power and Paradox of the Self-Deceiving Brain*. New York: W. W. Norton.
3. Solnit, Rebecca. 2018. *Call Them by Their True Names: American Crises (and Essays)*. Chicago, Illinois: Haymarket Books.

4. Havel, Václav. Quoted in Yates, Richard. 1975. *Disturbing the Peace*. New York: Delacorte Press/S. Lawrence.
5. Kaur, Valarie. 2020. *See No Stranger: A Memoir and Manifesto of Revolutionary Love*. First edition. New York: One World.

ACKNOWLEDGMENTS

I'm sure it'll come as no surprise to learn that I consider *The Weaver's Way* itself to be the result of a herculean weaving effort, both in the contributions that make up the book itself as well as the network of family and friends who held and supported me in this undertaking. In fact, it feels somewhat disingenuous to claim the title of *author* when really, the recognition and acknowledgment should go to those listed here and many more besides.

First and foremost, I would like to express my deepest gratitude and respect to the elders and traditional custodians—past, present, and emerging—of all the places where this book is written and read.

Secondly, to those who have been instrumental in helping to bring this idea into being.

Antonio—after writing so many words, I'm still not certain I've found the right ones to thank you as you deserve. If it wasn't for your courage and your vision, your willingness to keep saying yes, and your deep trust in relationships—especially our relationship—I wouldn't be here. It is through you that I discovered my own life's work, and I don't think there is a greater gift that anyone can receive. Thank you.

Abigail and Loida—on behalf of everyone who will read this book, thank you for sharing your time, your knowledge, and your way of seeing the world. For my own part, thank you for your patience with my endless questions and sometimes clumsy way of asking. I am humbled by your strength, resilience, and determination. When I think of your story, I am filled with joy, trepidation, and gratitude. Joy that this story is finally being told in this way. Trepidation that I may not do it justice. Gratitude at being granted the opportunity to do so. *Maltiox.*

I'm grateful to those of you in the Weaver's Guild—Therese, Akaya, Patty, Topher, Richie, Haile, Ayla, and Joyce. Getting to learn more about you and your stories was one of the unexpected blessings of writing this book. I'm not generally an optimist, but my proverbial glass was so full it was overflowing while interviewing you; it was full of sparkling water owing to the many frissons of excitement I felt as we talked.

As I wrote up the interviews, I constantly found myself on the edge of my seat, shouting out, *Yes, this is it!!* I'm grateful for your time in letting me get to know you, ask you questions, and share your story, even as uncomfortable as I know that it made many of you feel. Thank you for who you are, what you do, and how you do it. Your work gives me hope and comfort that I—we—are not alone. That we are, indeed, the Weavers.

Then there are those who played a pivotal role in bringing this book to fruition and to whom I owe a special thank you. True to form, I launched into this project having no idea what I was doing or how I would do it and am humbled by the countless people who shared their knowledge, experience, and resources to guide me on my way.

To Kathy Ruhf and Michael Gordon. I've been calling you my early editors, but it's probably more accurate to call you my forever editors! I'm so grateful for your generous gift of time and knowledge and your willingness to wade through overly dense paragraphs to help tease out the threads of meaning. I also discovered during those early days that writing—at least for me—is a very vulnerable process. It is testament to your care and compassion that you were able to hold me in my vulnerability and encourage me to keep going, even while ever-so-gently convincing me that not every idea I've ever had needed to make it into these pages.

Thanks also to Lissa Cowan, my actual editor. You have a special skill for helping people believe they have a story worth telling and for shaping that into something worth hearing. I'm also mindful of the fact that you went above and beyond the role of an editor, and I'm deeply grateful for all of the additional guidance you provided on printing, publishing, marketing, promotion, contracts, interview etiquette, and Christmas presents for nieces and nephews!

A huge thanks also to Boni and the rest of the team at Ingenium Books. It felt wonderful to surrender myself up to your wisdom and guidance.

To Sherry Miller, Manuela Balett, and the Leopold Stiftung Foundation. Your generosity provided the foundation of support that enabled me to dedicate the time and resources to writing and publishing this book. This book exists because of you, and your commitment to a better, fairer future for all. Thank you.

The roughly two years it took me to write this book paralleled the period of time when COVID-19 was at its most disruptive. I was in Northern Italy in January 2020 when it all started (the book and the pandemic), and, unable to return to Guatemala, I found myself living as a COVID refugee first in Italy, then in my own home country. Unsure of what the future held, I decided to spend the indeterminate amount of time that I would be in Australia house-sitting. House-sitting is another example of the gift economy, an exchange built on trust and mutual giving, and I felt there was something deeply symbolic in honoring the gift ecology in this way while this book came into being. Wherever I went, people welcomed me with warmth and generosity into their homes.

Another unexpected blessing of this book was this opportunity to listen to stories of people and places I wouldn't otherwise have had the opportunity to have heard. And I discovered new connections and friendships in the most unlikely of places. To everyone that opened their homes and their hearts to me during this time, thank you for investing in a world built on trust not transaction.

Last but not least, there is a circle of women to whom I am forever grateful. You know—I hope—who you are. I carry your love like a shawl upon my shoulders, its weight and warmth a reminder of unquestioned safety, kindness, and caring. It is from you that I source my own courage, bravery, and determination. It is with you that I am constantly learning and unlearning, thinking and rethinking. For your constant care and attention, your steady stream of encouragement and motivation, your inquiry and questions. From the bottom of my heart, thank you.

To all of whom have contributed in some way to the rich tapestry of this storytelling, this belongs to you as much to me. Or perhaps better said, it belongs to us. Thank you.

Finally, let me acknowledge and pay my respects to you, dear Reader. As I said at the beginning of this book, without you there is no *we*. And without *we* there are no Weavers. But together, we *are* the Weavers.

About the Author

A weaver and facilitator of transformative leaders, organizations, movements, and ideas, Corrina Grace is a socially-driven entrepreneur, engineer, hybrid thinker, and sustainability leader. She has a master's degree in social innovation for sustainable development and has spent fifteen years as a practitioner living and leading in Central American communities facing extreme environmental degradation and economic poverty.

She is the cofounder of a UNESCO award-winning organization, SERES, where she serves as a board member and senior advisor.

An internationally recognized facilitator, Corrina has worked with communities and organizations in Africa, Australia, Europe, North America, and Latin America.

She brings an engineer's love for solving problems, a pioneering spirit, and an entrepreneurial mindset to everything she does, along with a deep and unwavering commitment to justice and equality for people and the planet.

BOOK CLUB / READER'S GUIDE

Dig deeper into The Weaver's Way framework and the concepts explored, or take it to your book club. Download your reader's guide today by visiting https://ingeniumbooks.com/weaversbookclub.

Printed in Great Britain
by Amazon

20424316R00140